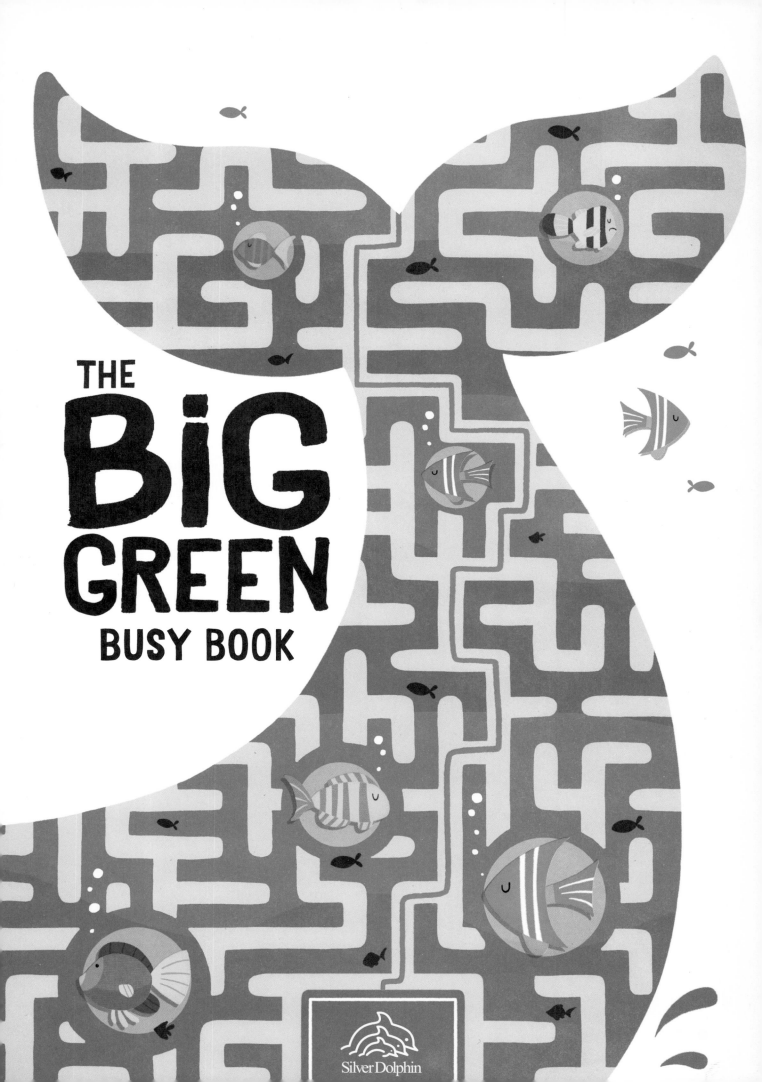

THE Big GREEN
BUSY BOOK

Silver Dolphin

ILLUSTRATED BY JOHN BIGWOOD,
GEORGIE FEARNS, ED MYER,
AND CHARLOTTE PEPPER

WRITTEN BY DAMARA STRONG
EDITED BY KATY LENNON
DESIGNED BY ZOE BRADLEY
COVER DESIGNED BY JOHN BIGWOOD

Silver Dolphin Books
An imprint of Printers Row Publishing Group
A division of Readerlink Distribution Services, LLC
10350 Barnes Canyon Road, Suite 100, San Diego, CA 92121
www.silverdolphinbooks.com

Printers Row Publishing Group is a division of Readerlink Distribution Services, LLC.
Silver Dolphin Books is a registered trademark of Readerlink Distribution Services, LLC.

All notations of errors or omissions should be addressed to Silver Dolphin Books Editorial
Department at the above address.

ISBN: 978-1-64517-318-2

Manufactured, printed, and assembled in Shaoguan, China.
First printing, March 2020. SL/03/20

24 23 22 21 20 1 2 3 4 5

PLANET-SAVING ACTIVITY FUN

Planet Earth is an awe-inspiring place that's home to many incredible plants and creatures—including you. But Earth is in danger—its climate is changing due to a rise in temperature. Some of this change is a result of what humans are doing. That's where YOU, eco-warrior extraordinaire, come in!

There are many ways to look after our planet, and it all starts with learning. These Earth-friendly puzzles and fascinating facts will teach you all about going green—from solar power and recycling to discovering where trash goes.

All the answers to the activities are at the back of the book. Get ready to puzzle your way to protecting the planet!

A GREEN WORD GUIDE

Here are some important terms that you will come across in the book:

Climate change: a significant change in the Earth's climate due to a rise in temperature. This is caused by high levels of a gas called carbon dioxide.

Global warming: the gradual rise in the Earth's temperature.

Greenhouse effect: the problem that is caused by too many greenhouse gases, such as carbon dioxide, methane, and ozone, in the air. The gases trap heat from the Sun and heat up the planet.

"Eco" or "green": something that doesn't harm the planet or is good for it.

ECO ISLAND

Take a trip to Eco Island, where you can relax, unwind, and unplug. People here love the outdoors and do their best to look after the land that they live on. Study the picture of the island below and then answer the questions.

The people on this island are "self-sufficient," which means they are able to make or produce anything that they need. They grow their own food, so they don't need to burn fuel to transport it from other places.

9

13

Solar panels and wind turbines turn sunlight and wind into unlimited energy for the island without releasing harmful gases and pollution.

QUESTIONS

1. Which animals are living in the forest on the west side of the island?

2. How many flags are on the island?

3. What is the sum of the numbers written on the kayaks in the sea around the island?

4. Are the vegetable patches in the north or the east?

5. How many wind turbines are on the island?

6. How many frogs are in or near the pond?

Challenge your friends and family to answer the questions from memory. Let them study the map for two minutes, then cover it up, and see how many questions they can answer correctly.

NECTAR DELIVERY

A busy bee has finished its morning nectar collection and is on its way back to the hive. Help the bee find its way through the hexagon maze to deliver its precious cargo.

Bees collect nectar from plants and turn it into honey in their stomachs. They bring it back to the hive, where it is stored in honeycomb.

START

FINISH

HONEY HUNT

These honeybees are hungry for nectar and are visiting a garden that is brimming with flowers.
Read the clues and match each one to the correct flower.

A.
Find a flower that is not purple or pink and has a center that's a different color from its leaves.

B.
Find a flower whose name is its color. It likes to sit in the shade and has petals with rounded edges.

C.
Find a plant with an animal in its name. It has more than one flower on its stem, and the flowers are looking up toward the Sun.

Plants need pollen from other flowers to reproduce. When a bee visits a flower, pollen gets stuck to its hairy body. It then transfers the pollen to the next flower that it lands on. This is called pollination. More than 30 percent of crops depend on pollinators such as bees.

Bees are sadly disappearing all around the world. One reason for this is that certain pesticides, which are used by humans to protect crops, are harming the bees. You can help by planting bee-friendly plants such as lavender and honeysuckle in your garden, so that bees have some tasty nectar to feast on.

-Catmint-

-Cowslip-

-Foxglove-

-Daffodil-

-Violet-

-Black-eyed Susan-

FOLLOW THE TRACKS

Yellowstone National Park is home to many different animals.
Follow the lines to see which track belongs to which creature.

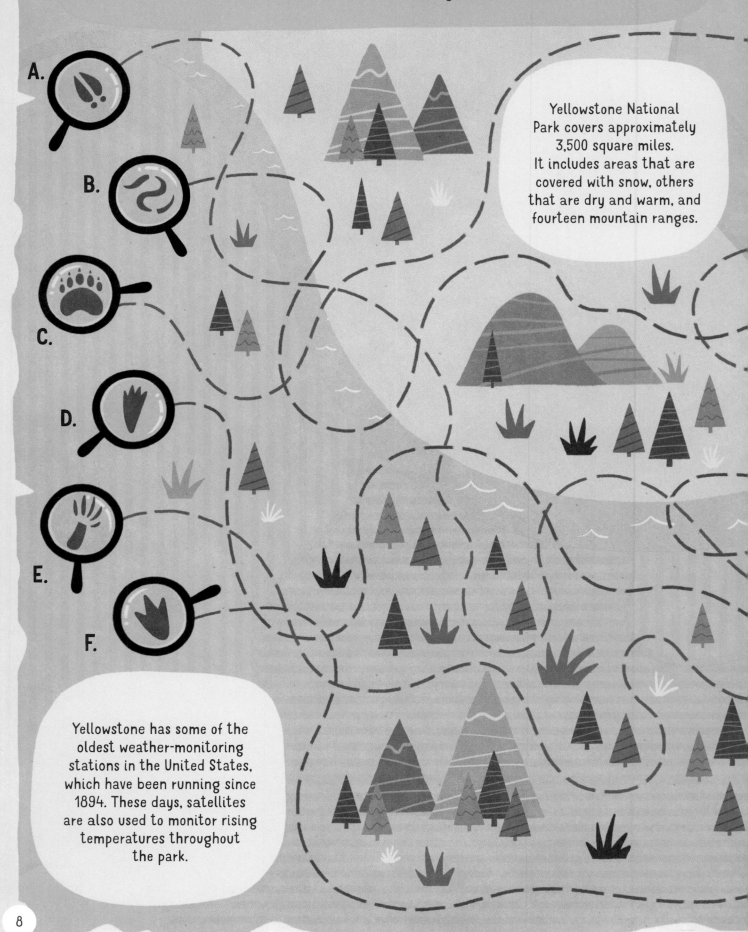

Yellowstone National Park covers approximately 3,500 square miles. It includes areas that are covered with snow, others that are dry and warm, and fourteen mountain ranges.

Yellowstone has some of the oldest weather-monitoring stations in the United States, which have been running since 1894. These days, satellites are also used to monitor rising temperatures throughout the park.

GRIZZLY BEAR

RED SQUIRREL

SNOWSHOE HARE

WHITE-TAILED DEER

MALLARD DUCK

RATTLESNAKE

Many animals and plants in Yellowstone are affected by climate change. Rising temperatures mean increased risks of forest fires and outbreaks of bark beetles, which harm trees.

RAIN FOREST RESIDENTS

This rain forest is buzzing with colorful animals and tropical plants. Count how many of each animal or plant you can spot from the checklist, then add up your answers. Does your total match the one shown?

Around half of all plant and animal species in the world live in rain forests. Everything that lives in them has adapted to the hot, damp, and often dark environment.

CHECKLIST

MONSTERA LEAVES

MACAW PARROTS

COCOA PODS

ORCHIDS

POISON DART FROGS

TOTAL = 43

The Amazon Rainforest in South America is the largest in the world. However, it is the forest that has lost the most trees due to deforestation. One of the many reasons that trees are cut down in the Amazon is to make space for cattle to graze.

FIND THE FOSSIL FUEL

Fossil fuels, such as oil and coal, are created deep within the Earth. They are dug up and burned as fuel to power everything from cars to light bulbs. Complete the fossil fuel facts below by filling the gaps with the correct words from the list.

FOSSIL-FUEL FACTS

1. Coal is formed when _____ die. They become buried in the ground and squashed into _____.

2. Around ___ of the world's energy comes from fossil fuels.

3. Natural gas has no smell but can be dangerous. A substance called mercaptan is added to it to make it smell like _____ ____, so it is easier to detect.

4. At the rate that humans are currently using it up, it is estimated that the reserves of ___ will run out by the year 2052.

5. The burning of fossil fuels for energy releases _____ _____, which causes global warming.

6. Nuclear power stations generate cheap energy but are very expensive to build. They also create dangerous _____ _____.

7. Oil is formed by plankton, _____, and other matter that sank and was buried at the bottom of the ocean.

8. Crude oil is used to make _____.

9. In America, _____ ___ is the fuel that is most often used to produce electricity.

10. _____ _____ is a renewable energy source, which means it will never run out.

WORD LIST

RADIOACTIVE WASTE	SOLAR POWER
PLANTS	GASOLINE
ROCK	CARBON DIOXIDE
NATURAL GAS	ALGAE
80%	ROTTEN EGGS
OIL	

Fossil fuels are non-renewable, which means that once they are gone we cannot make any more.

Oil is extracted from the Earth by drilling down into the ground. Many oil wells are made in the ocean so that oil can be drilled out from the rocks beneath the seabed.

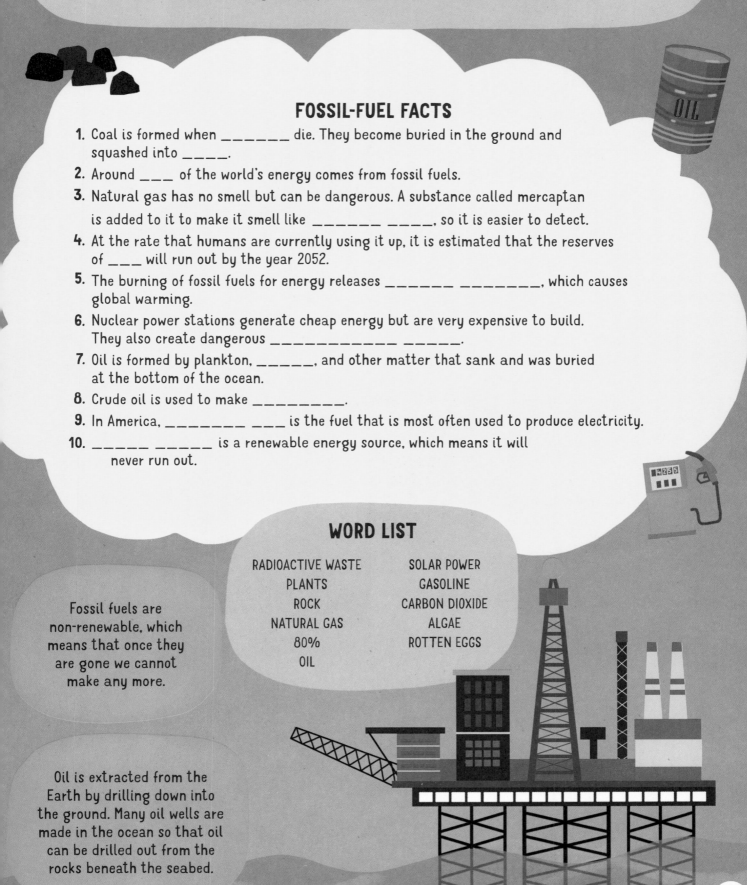

RECYCLING BINGO

This kitchen is full of trash, but a lot of it can be recycled or composted. Search the kitchen for all of the items pictured on the bingo cards on the opposite page. Time yourself to see how quickly you can find them, or challenge a friend to a recycling race!

Recycling is a great way to be eco-friendly. It stops waste from going to landfills and also reduces the need to make completely new products. Making new products uses a lot of energy and materials, and can create pollution.

METAL, GLASS, AND PLASTIC

SOUP CAN	PLASTIC WATER BOTTLE	SODA CANS
GLASS JAR	FOIL TRAY	KETCHUP BOTTLE
TUNA CAN	GLASS BOTTLE	JUICE CONTAINER

A great rule to remember is: reduce, reuse, recycle. By reducing the number of things that you use, reusing containers (such as bottles), and recycling, you save money, energy, and the environment.

PAPER, CARDBOARD, AND FOOD WASTE

APPLE CORE	CEREAL BOX	ENVELOPES
BANANA PEEL	EGGSHELLS	MAGAZINES
POTATO PEELS	CARDBOARD TUBE	NEWSPAPER

Every ton of paper that is recycled saves seventeen trees, 370 gallons of oil, and more than 8,100 gallons of water. That's enough energy to power a house for almost a year!

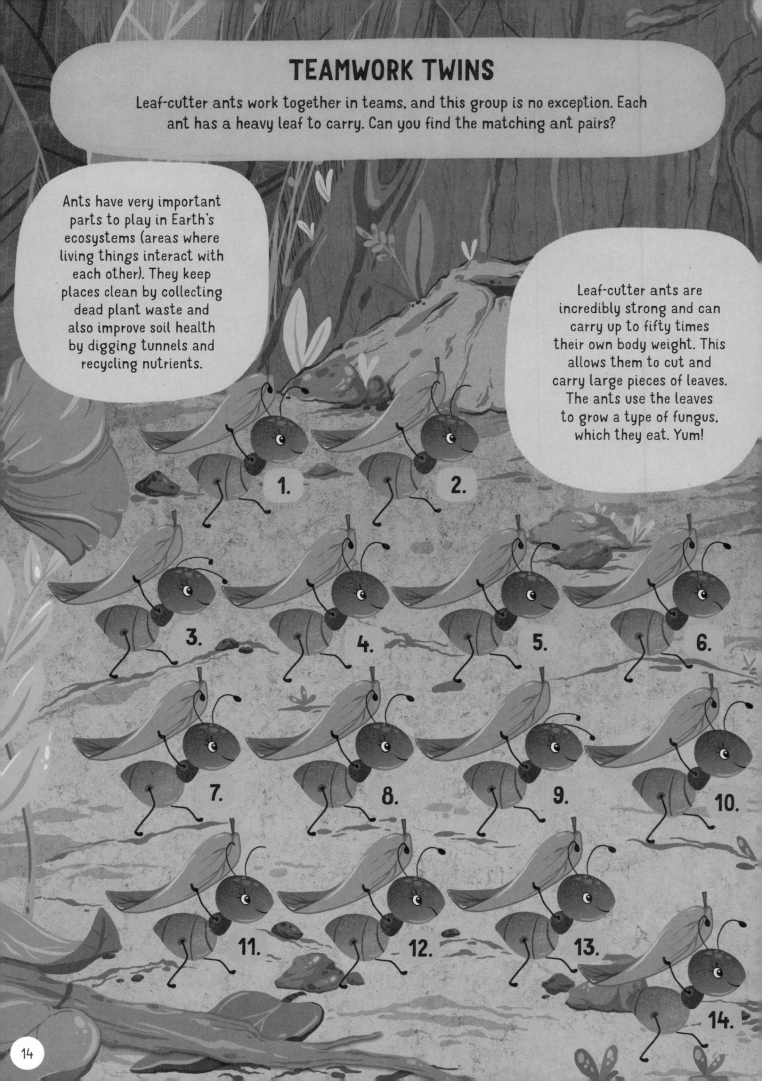

BUTTERFLY BRILLIANCE

Most butterflies have symmetrical wings, which means that if you laid one wing on top of the other, the patterns and colors would match exactly. Color in the butterfly below to make both of the wings match.

Many types of butterflies have been severely affected by climate change. The warming planet is impacting their life cycles and causing them to come out of their cocoons earlier. They have also started migrating at different times in the year, which means that there isn't as much food available when they arrive.

Global warming isn't all doom and gloom for our butterfly friends. Some species, such as Orange-tip butterflies and Silver-spotted skippers, have expanded their habitats. They are exploring new areas that were previously too cold for them.

CORAL REEF HIDE-AND-SEEK

This coral reef is full of colorful sea life. Count how many of each animal or plant you spot from the checklist, then add up your answers. Does your total match the one shown?

CHECKLIST

LEAFY SEA DRAGONS

LIONFISH

SEA FAN CORALS

GARDEN EELS

CHRISTMAS TREE WORMS

MIMIC OCTOPUSES

TRUMPETFISH

TOTAL = 47

Humans are currently the biggest threat to coral reefs. One major problem is pollution, which causes the water to become more acidic. Scientists believe that by 2085 oceans could be so acidic that coral might begin to dissolve.

Marine creatures aren't the only ones who depend on coral reefs to survive. Humans use coral reefs for food, tourism, and medicines.

Many different sea creatures and plants live near or in coral reefs. More than 25 percent of all marine life use reefs for food and shelter.

PLUMBING PRO

Help the plumber fix the leaking pipe. Fill the gaps by choosing the correct pieces from the selection on the left, so that water from the toilet can be washed straight to the sewer.

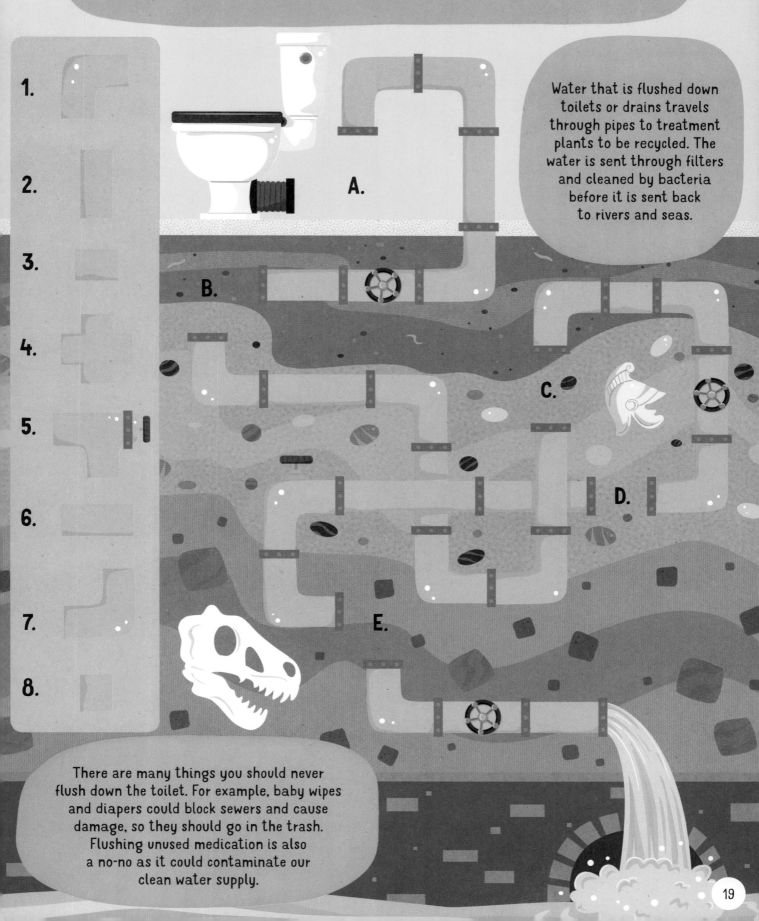

Water that is flushed down toilets or drains travels through pipes to treatment plants to be recycled. The water is sent through filters and cleaned by bacteria before it is sent back to rivers and seas.

There are many things you should never flush down the toilet. For example, baby wipes and diapers could block sewers and cause damage, so they should go in the trash. Flushing unused medication is also a no-no as it could contaminate our clean water supply.

FLOWER POWER

A living wall is a wall that has been covered with live plants and flowers. Can you spot the ten differences between the living wall below and the one on the opposite page?

Living walls, also known as green walls, aren't just for decoration. The roots of the plants support the wall, helping to keep it strong and stable.

The plants in living walls help clean the air by taking in harmful gases, such as carbon monoxide, and exchanging them for oxygen.

Living walls reduce noise pollution. They absorb sound, making noisy places, such as shopping centers or airports, quieter.

GOING CAMPING

Circle the group of images below that includes
all of the parts you need to make this picture of a tent.

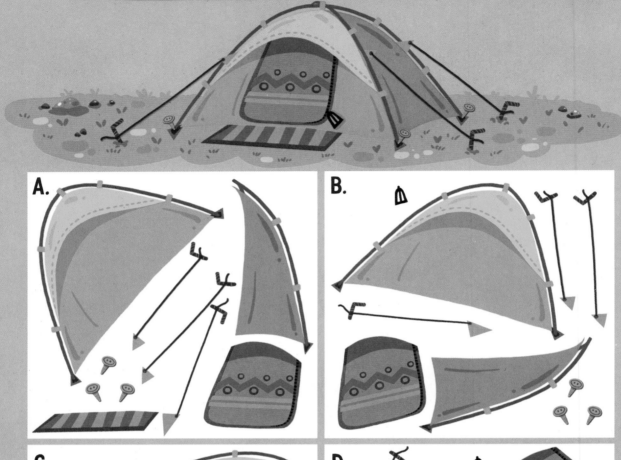

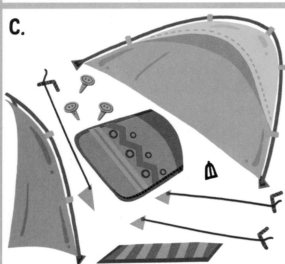

A.

B.

C.

D.

Over half of the world's animal
species live in forests, so it is
important to "Leave No Trace"
when you visit. If you go camping
or for a hike, never leave food
or litter behind.

Going camping is a great way
to unplug and get back to nature.
Sleeping outdoors and away from
artificial light can make people
feel more alert and more energetic.
Walking and hiking are also
great exercise.

TENT TROUBLE

These grid puzzles are real brainteasers. Follow the instructions to complete each one by pitching tents in the correct squares.

INSTRUCTIONS

Draw tents in the squares so that every tree has at least one tent horizontally or vertically next to it.

No tent can be next to or diagonal to another tent, nor can it be diagonal to any tree.

The numbers beside each row and below each column tell you how many tents they contain.

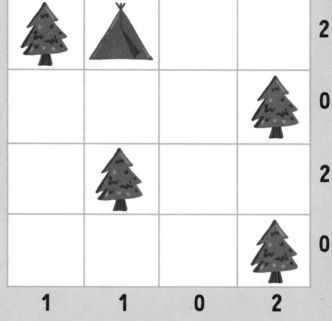

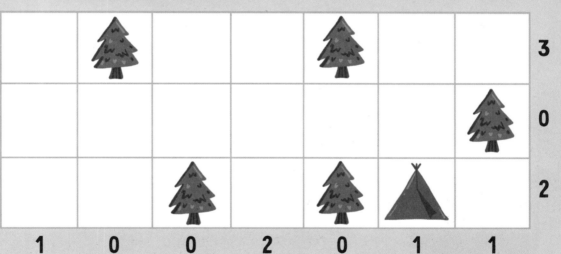

When setting up camp, try to disturb the land as little as possible. If your bed is bumpy or uneven, don't dig to level the land. Instead, put clothes under your sleeping bag to make it more comfortable.

Keep your campfires small. If you make a fire to cook food or keep warm, only use sticks found on the ground that can be broken by hand. Use water to put out the fire and make sure that it is completely out before you leave it.

GREEDY WORM

Worms eat food leftovers and paper and turn them into compost. Guide this hungry worm through the maze to the food pile, making sure it eats all the food and paper along the way. Be sure to avoid rocks and tin cans that block the path.

START

Composting is the decomposition, or rotting away, of natural waste, such as food scraps and grass trimmings. With the help of worms, this waste can be turned into nutrient-rich soil—a natural fertilizer for gardens.

Approximately 30 percent of the waste that is thrown away can be composted. This includes certain food, grass, and weeds. Compost keeps waste out of landfills where it would take up space and emit greenhouse gases.

Try setting up a compost heap. Select a dry, shady area and add equal amounts of brown materials, such as dead leaves, and green material, such as grass clippings. Water it regularly to keep it moist, and fill it with food scraps and helpful worms.

FINISH

25

PATCHWORK FASHION

These old clothes have been recycled to make a patchwork quilt.
One item from the clothesline hasn't been used. Which one?

People are buying more clothes than they used to and at cheaper prices. This is called "fast fashion." Human-made textiles often harm the planet because the process to make them can use toxic chemicals. It is also bad for the environment when they are thrown away.

SHOPPING SPREE

Buying second-hand clothes is a great way to get a new outfit without harming the planet. Read the questions below and see what you can afford from the thrift shop's window display.

OPEN

$7.00

$7.00

$3.00

$6.00

$4.50

$5.00

$6.50

$2.50

$7.00

Tons of unwanted clothing is sent to landfills every year. People are now being encouraged to recycle and buy second-hand. This reduces the need for new clothes to be made.

Many new, ingenious, and eco-friendly ways of making clothes are being tested. Some brands only use organic material, such as organic cotton, and others have even found a way to make clothes from old plastic bottles.

QUESTIONS

1. You have $15. How much money would you have left if you bought the jeans and blue sweater?

2. What's the largest number of items that you could buy with $15, which would leave you with no change?

3. If you had $20 and decided to buy the suitcase and the high heels, could you also afford the jeans?

SCHOOL CARPOOL

A carpool is a group of people who are all going to the same place, traveling together in one car. Follow the directions below to collect your friends on the way to school and then answer the questions about what you see on the journey.

DIRECTIONS

1. Start at home in the bottom left-hand corner.
2. Get in the car with whoever is driving you to school and pick up your friends from house number four.
3. Immediately turn left, then go left again.
4. Turn right just after the cafe, then right again at the end of the street.
5. Wait at the traffic light, then turn left when the light turns green.
6. Drive around the park and then into the school parking lot.

Vehicles emit gases that are harmful to the environment and humans. Cars, buses, and trucks produce 74 percent of carbon dioxide emissions around the world. This is the main contributor to global warming.

Café Clothes TOY STORE

START

1   2   3   4   5

TURN OFF YOUR ENGINE WHILE YOU WAIT

SCHOOL

Carpooling reduces the number of cars on the road, the amount of fuel used, and the quantity of greenhouse gases emitted. If it's safe, walking or riding your bike is an even more environmentally friendly way to get to school!

LIBRARY

HOSPITAL

QUESTIONS

1. How many houses are on your street?
2. How many bikes do you see from your car on your way to school?
3. Which shop is two down from the café?
4. How many ducks are on the pond?
5. How many buses can you see?

TURBINE TEST

Study this picture of a wind farm for one minute, then cover
it up and answer the questions below from memory.
Be as quick as you can, but don't get in a spin over it!

Since ancient times, humans have used
windmills to pump water and grind
up grains. Today, we also use wind
turbines to generate electricity.

QUESTIONS

1. How many wind turbines are there?
2. How many clouds are in the sky?
3. What color is the tractor?
4. How many blades does each turbine have?
5. What surrounds one of the turbines?

Wind turbines can reach as
high as a 20-story building
with blades as long as 200
feet. A large wind turbine can
power up to 600 American
homes for a year.

WASTE OF ENERGY

The truck needs to collect trash from each of the nine cans below. Draw the route the trash truck can take using just four straight lines. You cannot take your pen off the page and you must pass over every can. You also cannot go back along any of the lines you have already made, but you can cross over them.

Although not all trash can be recycled, some of it can be burned to create energy. Burning waste at high temperatures generates steam, which can move turbines and produce energy. It is a great way to reduce greenhouse gases and cut down on waste going into landfills.

START

Many countries are trying to become "zero waste" nations by recycling as much as possible or turning waste into energy.

HURRY HATCHLINGS

The newly hatched sea turtles need to get to the ocean. Can you guide them safely to the water, avoiding the paths blocked by plastic debris?

FINISH

Hatchlings can easily become trapped by debris. One study has found that two out of three will encounter plastic debris on their way to the water.

Trash is not the only thing for these baby turtles to be wary of. As they dash from their nest to the ocean, they are also in danger of being caught by predators, such as seabirds.

Sea turtles and other marine creatures sometimes mistake plastic for food. A plastic bag, for example, can look a lot like a jellyfish floating in the ocean.

START

ODD TURTLES OUT

There are three sea turtles below that are different from the others. Can you spot them?

MISSION TO SPACE

Exciting expeditions into space have taught humans a vast amount about our solar system, but they have also left quite a mess! The area around Earth is littered with junk, and it needs cleaning up. Follow the instructions to collect the trash.

Space junk can be a big problem. It travels at speeds of up to 17,400 miles per hour, which causes a lot of damage if it crashes into a satellite or the International Space Station, which is in orbit around the Earth.

There are many thousands of pieces of space junk orbiting the Earth. Any piece larger than 2 inches can be tracked from Earth, but there are many that are so small that it would be almost impossible to catalog everything.

A.

B.

C.

D.

E.

1.

2.

3.

4.

Many cleanup operations have been proposed to rid Earth's orbit of debris. Some of these missions plan to use harpoons and nets to gather the junk. Others hope to push it away using a gun with an electron beam.

INSTRUCTIONS

1. Start at the square with the coordinates C2 and collect the broken satellites.
2. Move one square to the right and then two squares down. What do you find?
3. Next, move three squares up and two squares right. What are the coordinates of this square, and what do you collect?
4. Now collect the nuts and bolts. How many squares and in which direction do you need to move to get there?
5. Which item has not been collected, and what are its coordinates?

5.   6.   7.

SEED SHUFFLE

Can you match these plants to their seeds?
Read the clues for help if you get stuck.

POPPY
The seeds of this plant grow in a pod.

PUMPKIN
This vegetable has seeds that are large and flat.

A.

B.

C.

SUNFLOWER
This flower's seeds are stripy.

D.

PINE TREE
The seeds belonging to this tree are inside cones.

E.

OAK TREE
Oak tree seeds look like they are wearing hats.

F.

MAPLE TREE
The seeds of this tree twirl as they fall to the ground.

We rely on plants to make oxygen for us, so the more plants the better! To reproduce, plants spread seeds, which grow into new plants.

36

GARDEN GRIDS

Fill in the two sudoku grids with these six types of flower. Each row, column, and six-square block must only contain one of each type.

1.

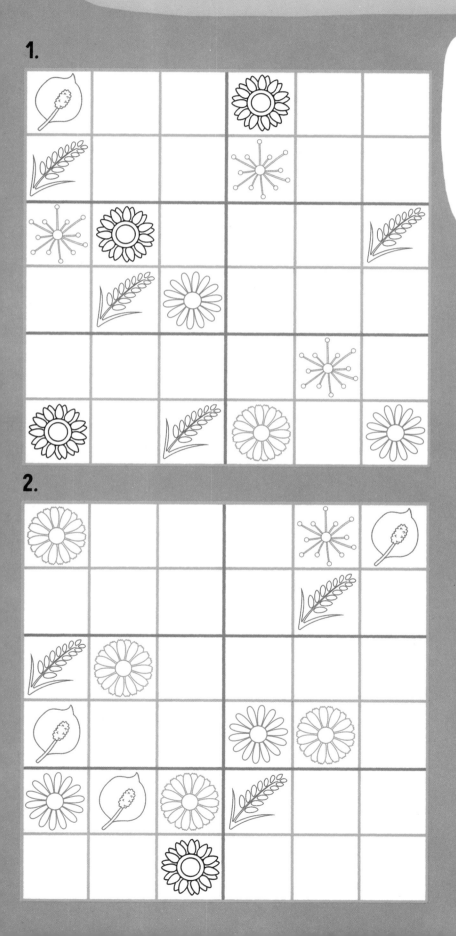

FLOWERS

MARIGOLD   DAISY   DANDELION

LAVENDER   PEACE LILY   SUNFLOWER

EXAMPLE:

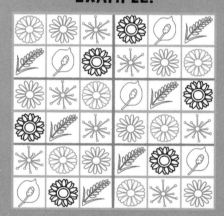

2.

Flowers have many different uses—from trapping pests to brightening your mood. Sunflower seeds make a tasty snack and are full of vitamins that are good for your body.

Peace lilies make perfect houseplants. They are good for your health because they purify the air by removing toxins with their leaves.

SOLAR SCRIBBLES

Draw stars on 50 percent of the blank solar panels below.
Then draw circles on 20 percent of the remaining blank panels. Finally,
draw swirls on 75 percent of the remaining solar panels.
How many solar panels are left blank?

Solar power is generated by solar panels, which collect energy from the Sun and convert it to heat or electricity. Solar energy is renewable, which means that it will never run out.

The energy that the Earth receives from the Sun is 10,000 times more than we can actually use. Our technologies are not yet advanced enough to harness all of this power, but it is hoped that one day they will be.

ON YOUR MARKS . . .

These children are having a race in the park. Follow the paths to see who wins. What medals do the others win?

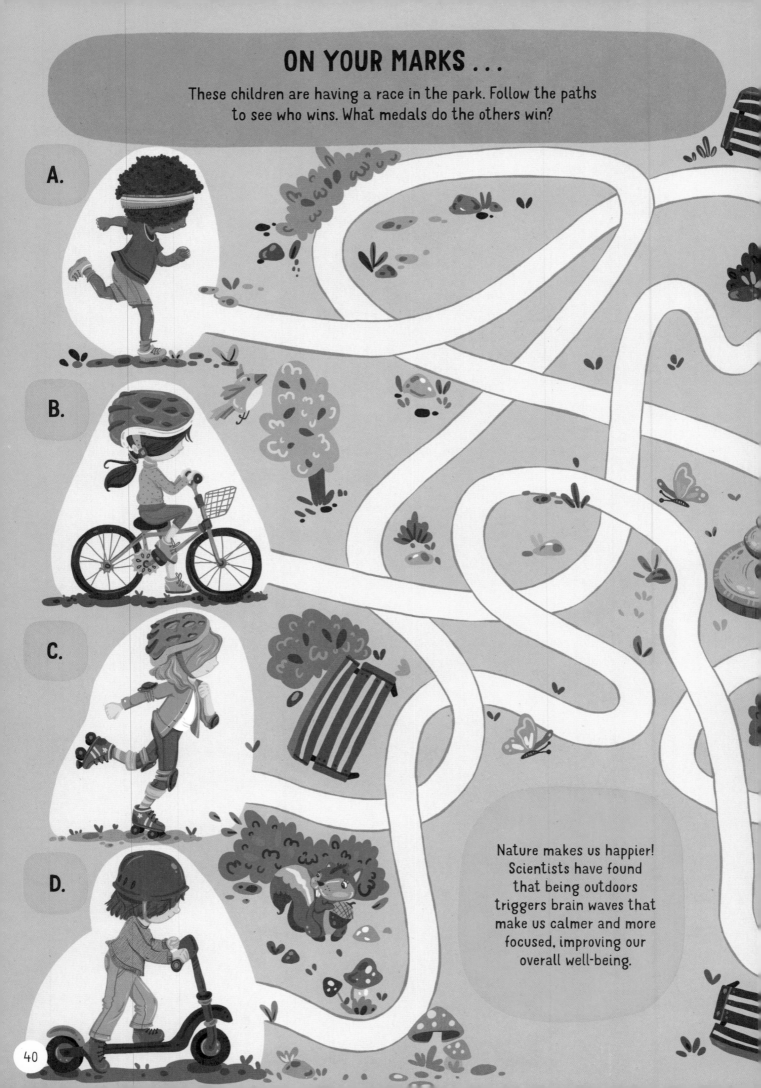

A.

B.

C.

D.

Nature makes us happier! Scientists have found that being outdoors triggers brain waves that make us calmer and more focused, improving our overall well-being.

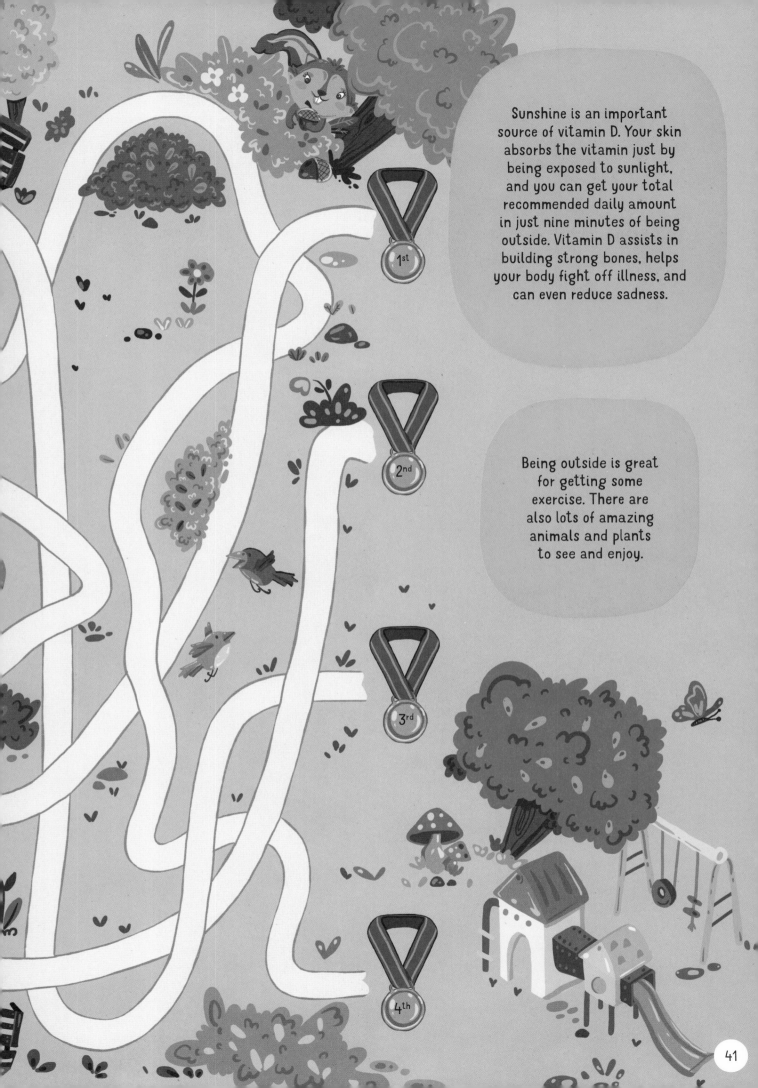

Sunshine is an important source of vitamin D. Your skin absorbs the vitamin just by being exposed to sunlight, and you can get your total recommended daily amount in just nine minutes of being outside. Vitamin D assists in building strong bones, helps your body fight off illness, and can even reduce sadness.

Being outside is great for getting some exercise. There are also lots of amazing animals and plants to see and enjoy.

1st

2nd

3rd

4th

AMAZING ARCTIC

Which of the tiles below are from the Arctic scene on the right-hand page?

The Arctic is at the northernmost part of the planet. It is home to some amazing wildlife, such as polar bears, seals, orcas, narwhals, and walruses.

A.

B.

C.

D.

E.

The ice in the Arctic contains about 10 percent of the world's fresh water. The ice reflects sunlight, which helps the region stay cool. It has an important role in keeping the Earth's climate stable.

F.

Global warming causes the ice on the Arctic to melt and shrink. This is happening too rapidly for the animals of the Arctic to adapt. Habitats are quickly being lost, and food is becoming harder to find.

G.

H.

I.

J.

Melting ice also speeds up global warming. As the ice slowly disappears, it reflects less sunlight, causing the surrounding oceans to heat up.

FROG HOPPING

Help the frog cross the pond. He can only jump on lily pads with numbers from the three times table on them. Can you find the correct path?

FINISH

Ponds provide many animals with places to drink, cool off in hot weather, and find food. However, many ponds are at risk of pollution because rain washes pesticides, fertilizers, and gasoline from roads into the water.

Frogs are amphibians, which means that they live in and around water. They need to be near fresh water to keep their skin wet and to lay eggs. Some frogs can jump over twenty times their own body length.

24
16
30
38
19
36
21
12
5
17
24
9
10
18
29
27
34
14
15
13
7
3
26
22
4
11
8

START

44

FRESH FOOD FEAST

Take a trip to the farmers' market to buy some fresh, local produce.
Read the prices on all the items and then answer the questions.

Shopping at a farmers' market is a great way to be green. The produce doesn't travel very far from its source, saving fuel and reducing greenhouse gas emissions.

FLOWERS
$5 PER BUNCH

APPLES
5 FOR $1

LEMONS
30¢ EACH

CARROTS
10 FOR $1.50

TOMATOES
6 FOR $1

ZUCCHINI
3 FOR $2

BEETS
50¢ EACH

CAULIFLOWERS
$1 EACH

CORN
50¢ EACH

Fresh food that is bought at a supermarket often comes wrapped in plastic. This keeps it fresh while it is transported. Shopping at a farmers' market cuts down on this plastic waste because the food doesn't need to be wrapped up.

HONEY AND JAM $2.50 EACH

BREAD $2 PER LOAF

ORANGES 50¢ EACH

LETTUCE $1 EACH

WATERMELONS $3.50 EACH

PUMPKINS $3 EACH

POTATOES 2 FOR 50¢

QUESTIONS

1. You have $10. If you bought ten carrots, three cauliflowers, and four beets, how much change would you get?

2. If you started with $15 and you bought a pumpkin, two loaves of bread, three zucchini, and ten apples, would you have enough money left to get a bunch of flowers?

3. You want to make a vegetable stew and a lemon dessert. How much would it cost to buy ten carrots, three zucchini, a pumpkin, six tomatoes, four potatoes, and four lemons?

Many foods that are sold at farmers' markets are organic. This means that they are grown without using chemical fertilizers or pesticides.

POLAR BEAR REFLECTIONS

Can you figure out which image below shows the correct reflection of the polar bear at the top of the page?

Researchers predict fewer than 10,000 polar bears will remain by 2050 if Arctic sea ice continues to melt due to climate change. That would mean a 66 percent loss in the polar bear population since 2001.

Polar bears are made for the Arctic. They have nonslip foot pads and strong legs with large, flat paws to help them walk on ice and swim in the freezing Arctic waters.

A.

B.

C.

D.

EGG COUNT

These penguins are getting ready to lay some eggs. If each penguin with yellow feet lays one egg and each penguin with orange feet lays two eggs, how many eggs will be laid altogether?

Some gentoo penguins live on small islands near Antarctica. Recently, life there has become more difficult. Pollution in the sea and overfishing by humans means that there is not as much food for the penguins as there was previously.

Gentoo penguins spend most of their time on land, but they swim near shore to catch food, which includes fish, squid, and krill. They can stay underwater for up to seven minutes and swim as deep as 655 feet.

MUSEUM MEMORY MUDDLE (PART ONE)

This museum has an exhibition of extinct animals on display. These majestic creatures once walked the Earth, swam the seas, or flew through the air, but sadly they no longer exist. Study the creatures for one minute and then turn the page and see how many of their names you can remember.

MOA

QUAGGA

WESTERN BLACK RHINOCEROS

GOLDEN TOAD

PASSENGER PIGEON

TASMANIAN TIGER

The Tasmanian tiger of Australia was a mostly nocturnal creature, coming out at night to hunt for food. Its extinction was caused by human hunters and climate change.

WOOLLY MAMMOTH

GREAT AUK

The woolly mammoth became extinct about 4,300 years ago. It lived in extremely cold environments, but had thick fur to keep it warm. Global warming and hunting may have caused its extinction.

TECOPA PUPFISH

PYRENEAN IBEX

DODO

STELLER'S SEA COW

The dodo was a flightless bird that lived on the island of Mauritius in the Indian Ocean. Scientists suspect it never developed the ability to fly because it had no known predators on the island until humans arrived.

MUSEUM MEMORY MUDDLE (PART TWO)

Write the names of as many animals as possible underneath their pictures.
Try to remember as much as you can without peeking at the previous page.

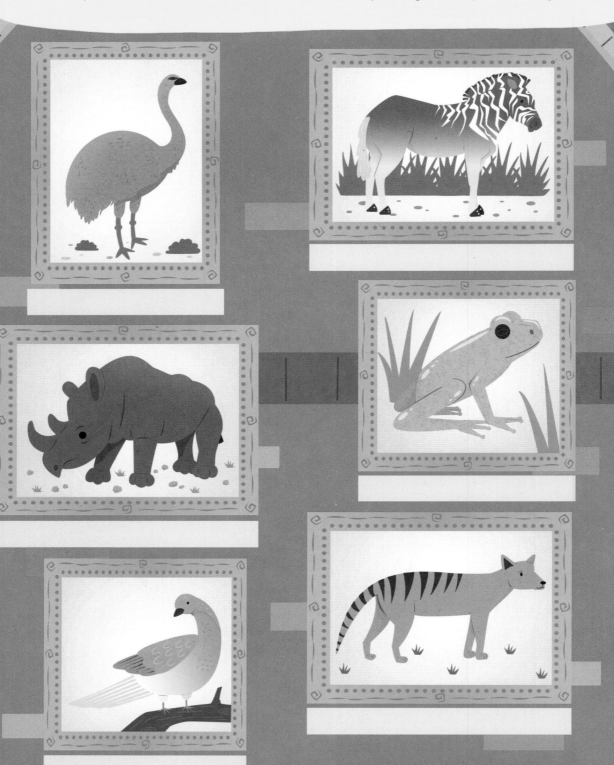

Extinction often occurs naturally, due to changes in the
environment or a natural disaster. However, it's possible
that the actions of humans are now causing the
extinction of species to happen a thousand times faster.

Currently, human activity is causing plants and animals to die off so quickly that scientists think we may be in the middle of the largest extinction event since the loss of the dinosaurs.

BONUS QUESTION
One picture has changed. Can you figure out which one?

WHO HOOKED THE BOOT?

Follow the fishing lines to find out which one leads to the boot.

Lots of trash ends up in our oceans—plastic especially. Many sea creatures mistake plastic items for food, which is dangerous to them and the creatures that eat them.

The Ocean Cleanup project uses advanced technology to rid the ocean of plastic waste. With a full-scale cleanup effort and a reduction in waste, the oceans could be plastic-free by 2050.

ODD FISH OUT

Each of these types of fish are in danger of disappearing from the oceans. Find the odd fish out in each shoal below.

Overfishing is when more fish are caught for food than can be replaced naturally.

Many fisheries use large nets with heavy weights to drag them across the seabed and pick up everything in its path. These nets destroy ocean habitats and pick up fish that shouldn't be caught.

GROUPER

HAKE

TUNA

Atlantic bluefin tuna are endangered. They are a delicacy in Asia, and one single fish once sold for over $3 million in Japan!

CROSSED WIRES

Saving energy is as easy as the flick of a switch, and everyone can do it at home by turning off lights when they are not needed. Follow the wires to find out which switch controls which lamp.

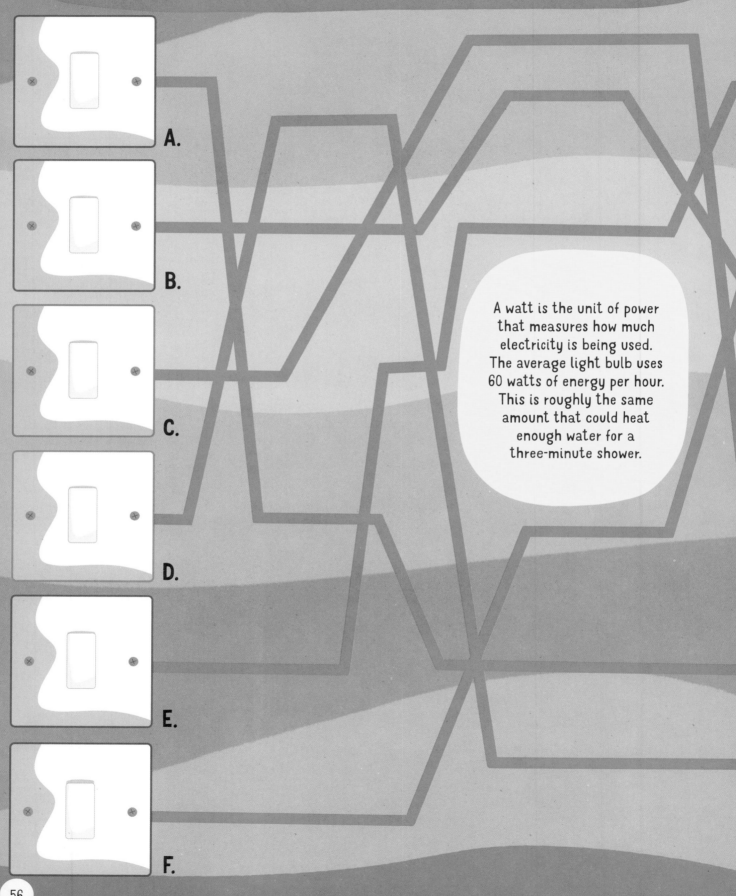

A.

B.

C.

A watt is the unit of power that measures how much electricity is being used. The average light bulb uses 60 watts of energy per hour. This is roughly the same amount that could heat enough water for a three-minute shower.

D.

E.

F.

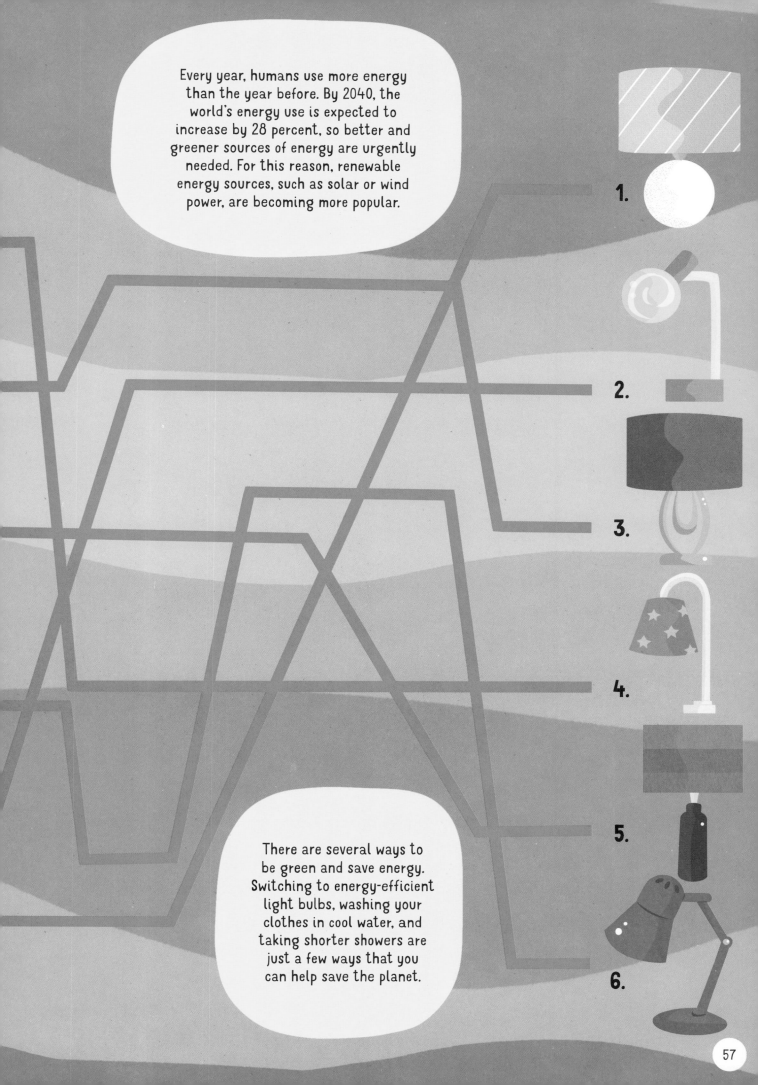

Every year, humans use more energy than the year before. By 2040, the world's energy use is expected to increase by 28 percent, so better and greener sources of energy are urgently needed. For this reason, renewable energy sources, such as solar or wind power, are becoming more popular.

There are several ways to be green and save energy. Switching to energy-efficient light bulbs, washing your clothes in cool water, and taking shorter showers are just a few ways that you can help save the planet.

1.

2.

3.

4.

5.

6.

SILHOUETTE SPOTTING

Leaves come in all shapes and sizes. Can you match the leaves to their silhouettes below?

MAPLE

OAK

BEECH

BIRCH

POPLAR

HAWTHORN

A.

B.

C.

D.

E.

F.

Leaves are a very important part of a plant. Their job is to absorb sunlight and carbon dioxide, which are used to create food for the plant. This process is called photosynthesis.

When trees are cut down, the carbon that is stored inside them is released into the air as carbon dioxide. This builds up in the atmosphere and contributes to global warming.

ANCIENT TREES

Bristlecone pine trees are extraordinary plants that can live for thousands of years. Read the clues below to discover which is the oldest tree in the image below, then answer the bonus questions.

The Methuselah tree in the White Mountains of California was thought to be the oldest living bristlecone pine at around an astonishing 4,850 years old. However, in 2012, it was beaten by a nearby bristlecone that was estimated to be 5,065 years old!

CLUES

1. The oldest tree is not the tallest.
2. It has more than six branches.
3. Its trunk is not straight.
4. It has leaves.

A.

B.

C.

D.

E.

The bristlecone pine is a protected species inside the National Parks of the United States. The locations of some of the oldest trees are even kept secret so that people can't find and accidentally harm them.

BONUS QUESTIONS

1. If the oldest tree in this scene is 5,000 years old and the youngest tree is 2,673 years younger, how old is the youngest tree?
2. The second-oldest tree is 2,351 years older than the youngest tree. How old is it?

VEGGIE PATCH VISITORS

This garden is packed full of tasty fruit and vegetables and has attracted lots of animal visitors who are looking for a snack. Find all of the critters from the checklist and add up your answers. Does your total match the one shown?

CHECKLIST

RABBITS

SNAILS

SLUGS

LADYBUGS

CROWS

TOTAL = 26

Pesticides are used to get rid of pests, mainly bugs, that destroy crops. However, pesticides can be dangerous for the environment. They can get into the water that's underground and harm the surrounding ecosystems.

By growing your own fruit and vegetables, you are more likely to eat a healthier diet and you can control the types of pesticides that your food comes into contact with.

While some insects are bad for crops, there are many that you do want to see in your garden. Earthworms work to improve the soil, and spiders get rid of pests that can kill your plants.

RECYCLED ROBOT

This cheerful robot is made from old computer parts. Find the box that contains all the correct parts that are needed to build it.

In 2016, 49.3 million tons of e-waste was disposed of worldwide. E-waste means electronic waste and includes computers, televisions, cell phones, and anything with a plug or battery.

Recycling 1 million laptops saves the same amount of energy that would be needed to power over 3,500 homes each year.

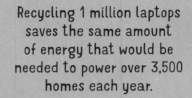

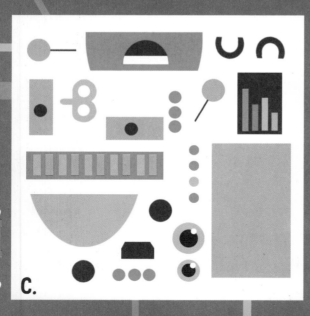

A.

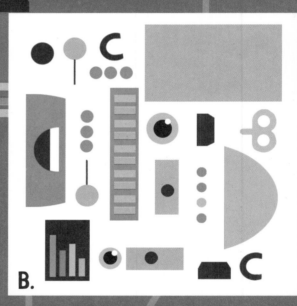

B.

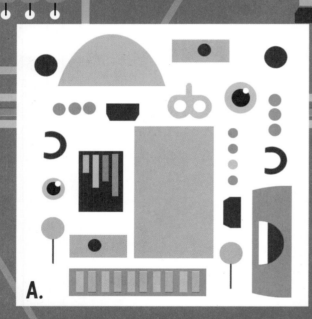

C.

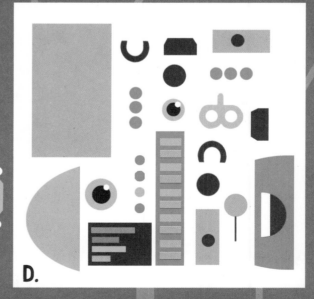

D.

E-WASTE ENIGMA

Be a recycling champion and complete these sudoku grids with the electrical items shown. Each row, column, and bold box in the grids can contain just one of each image.

1.

Instead of throwing away old electronic goods, check to see if you have a recycling center nearby. Shops that sell electronic items may also have recycling programs to responsibly dispose of e-waste.

2.

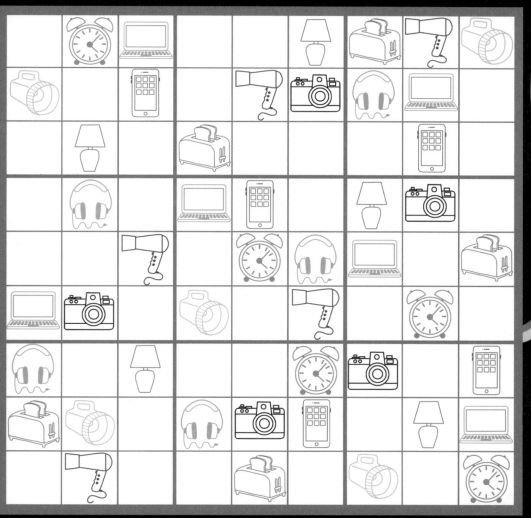

The amount of e-waste that is thrown away every year is equal to about two laptops per person.

STAR TO STAR

Look up into the night sky. What can you see? If you are in the countryside, you will be able to see lots of stars. These stars make shapes called constellations. Follow the instructions to complete these constellations. The first one has been done for you to show you how it works. You can find out the names of these constellations on the answer pages.

EXAMPLE:

INSTRUCTIONS

The dots for each constellation are a different color, and each dot has a set of arrows attached to it. Start at any dot and, using a ruler, follow the line in the direction that the arrow is pointing. You will reach a dot that has an arrow pointing along the same line. Connect these two dots together. Continue connecting dots in this way until there are no more arrows left. Remember to only connect arrows that match in color.

It can be difficult to see stars from a city or town because of "light pollution." This is when the night sky is lit up by artificial lights, such as street lights. The loss of natural light can be bad for humans as it affects their natural sleeping patterns. Some communities have started limiting the bright lights that they use to avoid too much light pollution.

Light pollution can have a big effect on animals. It causes some birds to migrate at the wrong time, missing the nesting season. It can also affect their eating and sleeping patterns. For example, city birds stay awake for much longer than country birds.

Sea turtle hatchlings are affected by artificial lights. When they emerge from their eggs, they look for the light of the Moon reflecting in the ocean. If there are other lights nearby, they do not know which direction to move in and do not always make it to the water.

PLASTIC POLLUTION

How many plastic bottles can you count in the jumble below?

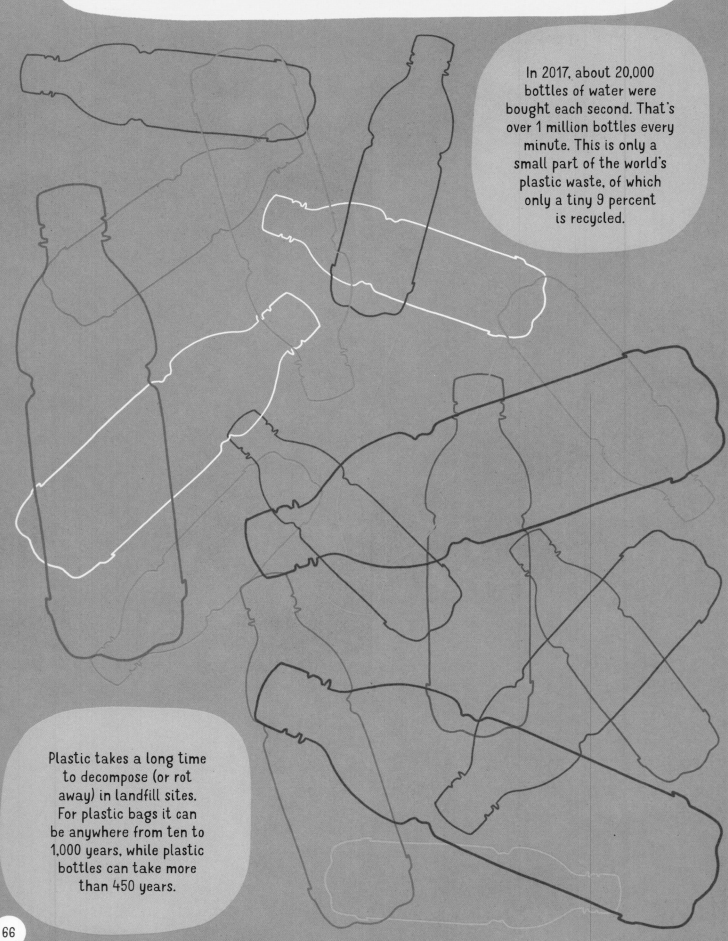

In 2017, about 20,000 bottles of water were bought each second. That's over 1 million bottles every minute. This is only a small part of the world's plastic waste, of which only a tiny 9 percent is recycled.

Plastic takes a long time to decompose (or rot away) in landfill sites. For plastic bags it can be anywhere from ten to 1,000 years, while plastic bottles can take more than 450 years.

CREEPY-CRAWLY CAPER

This log pile is home to lots of scuttling critters. Count how many of each bug from the checklist you can spot, then add up your answers. Does your total match the one shown?

CHECKLIST

- STAG BEETLES
- LADYBUGS
- GOLDEN STAG BEETLES
- CUCUMBER BEETLES
- SPIDERS
- CENTIPEDES
- DUNG BEETLES
- FRUIT BEETLES

TOTAL = 48

Climate change is causing outbreaks of beetles that destroy trees. This means less carbon dioxide is absorbed by the trees, which makes climate change worse.

Dung beetles use animal dung as food and to lay their eggs in. As they move through the dung they introduce oxygen to it, which stops it from creating harmful methane gas when it decomposes.

WORKING FOR THE PLANET

Many people do jobs that help save the planet. Answer the questions below to find out which green career would suit you.

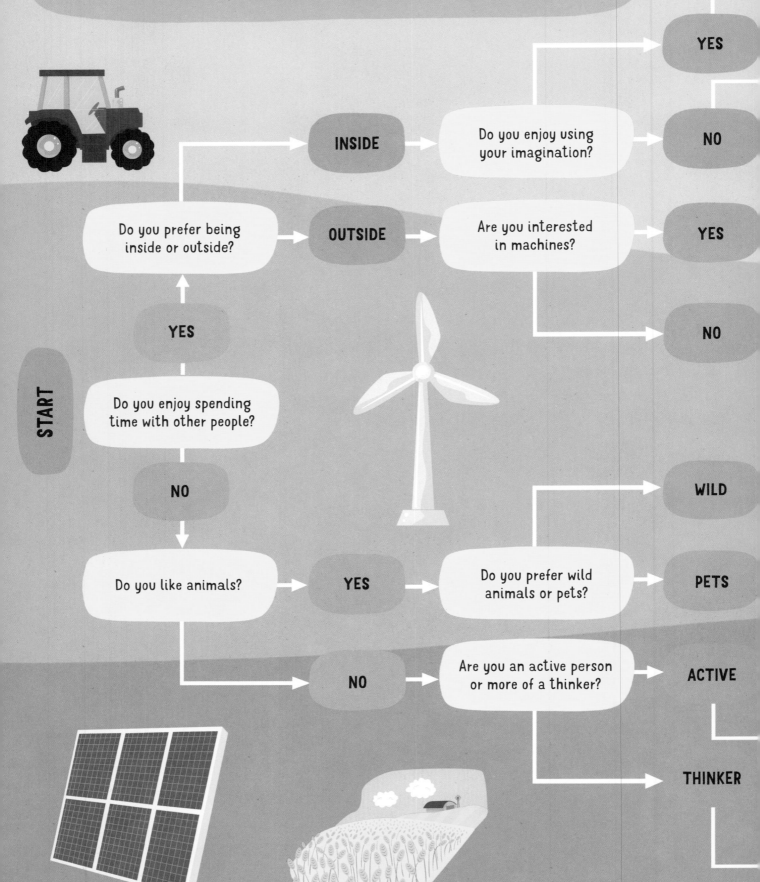

START

Do you enjoy spending time with other people?

YES → Do you prefer being inside or outside?

INSIDE → Do you enjoy using your imagination? → YES / NO

OUTSIDE → Are you interested in machines? → YES / NO

NO → Do you like animals?

YES → Do you prefer wild animals or pets? → WILD / PETS

NO → Are you an active person or more of a thinker? → ACTIVE / THINKER

Environmental Charity Officer
If you're creative and have a big imagination, you could become an environmental charity officer. You would be in charge of raising money and managing projects for your chosen green charity.

Environmental Lawyer
If you like to argue your point and stick to the facts, you could become an environmental lawyer. You would work to protect the planet by using the law to debate environmental matters with governments and companies.

Environmental Engineer
If you enjoy working outside and love big machines, you could become an environmental engineer. You would work to improve things such as recycling, waste disposal, and pollution control.

Environmental Science Technician
If you have a scientific mind, you could become an environmental science technician. You would monitor the environment and investigate sources of pollution by performing laboratory and field tests.

Wildlife Biologist
If you are scientific, practical, and passionate about animals, then a career as a wildlife biologist would be perfect for you. You would get to study animals, their behavior, and the impacts that humans have on them and their habitats.

Organic Farmer
If you love looking after animals and have a green thumb when it comes to plants, a farmer's life could be for you. You would raise animals and grow organic crops to sell.

Green Builder
If you're an active person who's good with their hands, you would make a great builder. By specializing in eco-friendly construction, you could be in charge of building eco-homes.

Recycling Officer
If you are good at solving problems, you could be a recycling officer. You would manage recycling schemes, inspect recycling sites, and give presentations to communities, encouraging people to recycle more.

BREAKAWAY ICEBERG

An iceberg has broken away from the glacier and is floating off into the ocean. Can you find which iceberg on the right matches the gap marked with a dashed line in the glacier on the left?

Glaciers are huge masses of ice that "flow" across land like very slow rivers. They form over hundreds of years when fallen snow is compressed and turns into ice.

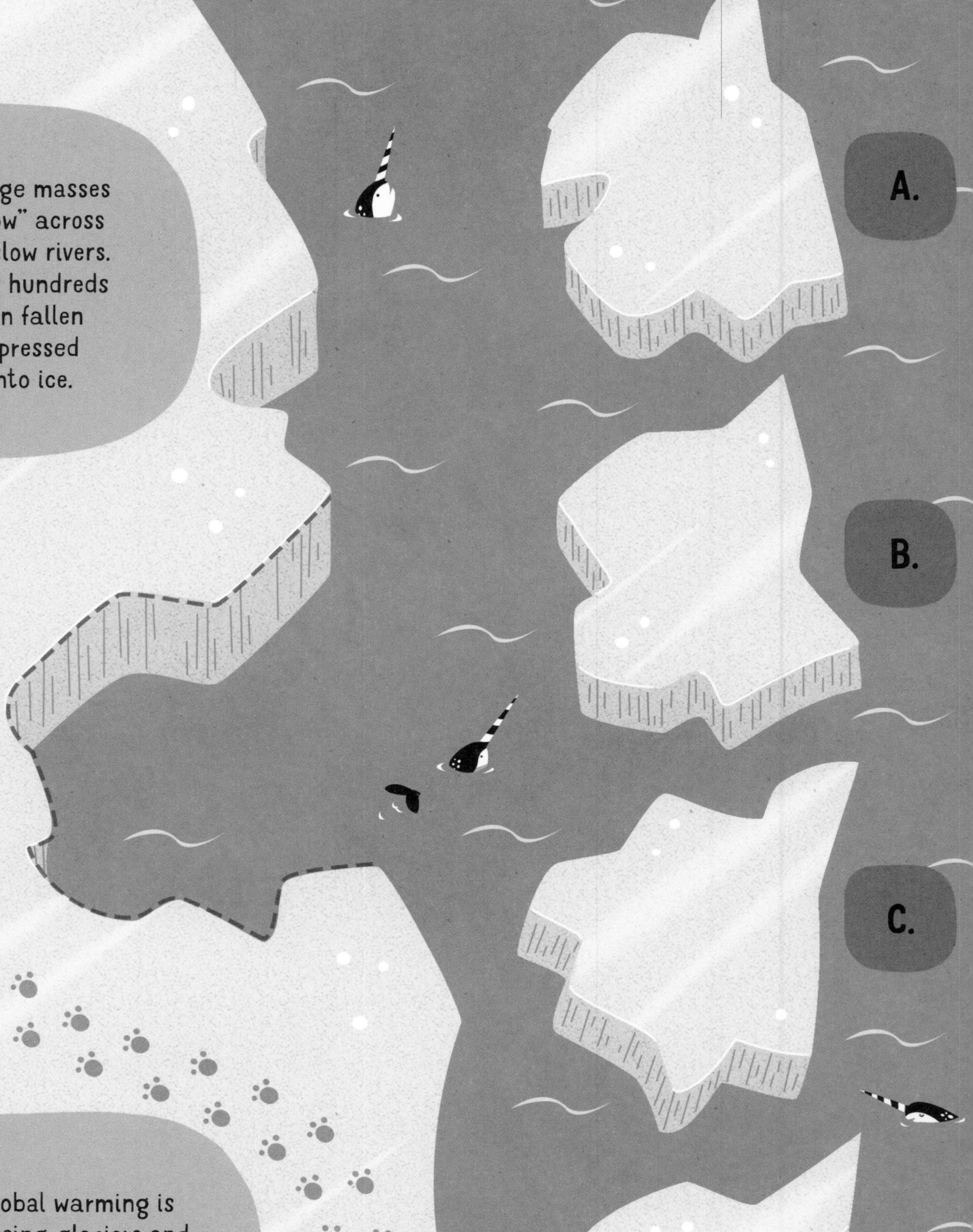

Global warming is causing glaciers and ice around the world to melt. This is making sea levels rise and increasing the risk of flooding.

A.

B.

C.

D.

FUN IN THE SNOW

Snowflakes are symmetrical—if you were to fold them in half, the sections would match exactly. Complete the snowflakes below by drawing in the missing sections so that they each have six branches.

Snowflakes form when an extremely cold drop of water attaches to a small particle in the sky, such as dust or pollen. It freezes and creates an ice crystal. As the ice crystal falls to the ground, water vapor freezes onto it, making new crystals and forming the six branches of the snowflake.

Climate change can trigger extreme weather events, including massive blizzards. In recent years, warming temperatures in the Arctic have moved the polar vortex, a wide area of cold, swirling air, southward to the United States. This has caused exceptionally cold temperatures.

KANGAROO CROSSING

Busy roads can be a dangerous problem for many animals. This kangaroo is trying to cross the road and get to the field. Can you find the path to guide her through the traffic jam, avoiding the spiky echidnas and plants blocking the way?

START

Kangaroos are found in Australia and New Guinea, and live and travel in small groups called mobs. They often gather along roadsides, searching for green grass to eat. This results in a dangerous situation for kangaroos and humans alike.

Animals all around the world are at risk from humans building near their habitats. In some places, wildlife crossings, such as grassy bridges, are built to give creatures a safe place to cross busy highways.

FINISH

In Canberra, Australia, local police estimate that over 2,000 kangaroos are hit by vehicles every year.

SPOTTER'S GUIDE

This forest is full of chirping birds hopping along the tree branches, and the bird-watchers are getting some great photos. Can you figure out which bird-watcher took which picture on the opposite page?

Bird-watching (also known as birding) is a very popular hobby in America. Birders are encouraged to always put the birds first and not disturb the animals or their habitat.

BLUE JAY

WHITE-BREASTED NUTHATCH

ROSE-BREASTED GROSBEAK

WOOD THRUSH

PURPLE FINCH

NORTHERN CARDINAL

Climate change is affecting how some birds migrate. Warm seasons are starting earlier and changing annual breeding and migration patterns. Meanwhile, winds are becoming stronger, making it more difficult for birds to travel to their destinations.

ON THE FARM

Which of the tiles below are not from the
farm scene on the right-hand page?

Farms are areas of land that
are used to grow crops, such as
grains, fruits, and vegetables,
and to raise animals, such as
cows, chickens, and pigs. Cows
are reared for dairy and meat,
and their skin is used to make
leather products. Historically,
they were also employed as
work animals to pull
carts and plow fields.

A. **B.**

C. **D.**

E.

To help our planet, some
farmers practice sustainable
farming. This means that
they try not to damage the
environment, and try to give
the animals a good quality of
life. This includes only using
natural fertilizers to keep soil
healthy and reduce pollution.
They let animals move around
freely rather than keeping
them in barns or cages.

F.

H.

G.

Many small family farms still
exist and stock stores with
organic (produced without
chemicals) dairy products,
meat, fruit, and vegetables.
Sometimes it can be difficult
for small farms to compete
with the prices of larger farms,
so it's great to shop at farmers'
markets to support them.

I. **J.**

Factory farming is farming on a large scale. Factory farmers raise huge amounts of livestock and often focus on making money rather than what is good for the animals. Although it produces a lot of food for a low cost, factory farming causes a lot of deforestation and air and water pollution.

ABOVE OR UNDERGROUND?

Do you know how things grow? Look at the images of the food below and decide if they grow above the ground or under the ground.

Vegetables are an important part of our diet. These plants provide nutrients that keep you healthy and strong.

CARROTS

CHICKPEAS

PEANUTS

POTATOES

BROCCOLI

WATERMELONS

RADISHES

PINEAPPLES

CASHEW NUTS

Root vegetables and tubers are both underground vegetables. Root vegetables are part of a plant's root, while tubers are enlarged stems that store nutrients for a plant to use in the winter.

THINK LIKE AN APE

Orangutans spend their time swinging around in the rain forests of Borneo and Sumatra in Southeast Asia. Sadly, their habitats are under threat by humans who are cutting down the trees to produce palm oil. Get up close and personal with these amazing apes by tackling the quick-fire quiz below.

1. The name "orangutan" comes from the Malay words "oran" and "utan," but what do they mean?

a. King of the swingers
b. Forest person
c. Orange monkey

2. What vital role do orangutans play in the life of the forest?

a. Gardener
b. Lumberjack
c. Personal trainer

3. When did scientists discover a third species of orangutan?

a. 1897
b. 1937
c. 2017

4. What physical characteristics do dominant male orangutans display?

a. Large pads on their cheeks
b. Black-and-orange striped backs
c. Short arms

5. How long are baby orangutans carried around by their mothers?

a. Up to three months
b. Up to eighteen months
c. Up to five years

6. Where do orangutans spend most of their time?

a. Walking on the forest floor
b. Swimming in rivers
c. Living in the tree canopy

Palm oil comes from the vegetable of the oil palm tree. Indonesia and Malaysia produce over 85 percent of the global supply of palm oil. In these areas, the rain forest is being cut down to allow for palm oil plantations.

7. Which of the following contains palm oil?

a. Pizza
b. Soap
c. Both of the above

Orangutans are very loud animals. They communicate using howls and bellows that can be heard far away. This yelling keeps other orangutans away from their territory.

WHAT A LOAD OF GARBAGE

This landfill is full of garbage. Count how many of each item you can spot from the checklist, then add up your answers. Does your total match the one shown?

CHECKLIST

 HAIR SPRAY CANS

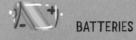 BATTERIES

 ALUMINUM CANS

 TELEVISIONS

 OLD CAR TIRES

 COFFEE MAKERS

TOTAL = 32

Landfills are areas of land where trash is dumped and covered with soil. They are really bad for the environment because as the trash decays it lets off harmful greenhouse gases. Toxic chemicals from electrical items can also leak into the surrounding soil and water.

Food, plastic, and paper products make up roughly half of all landfill waste. If more people composted and recycled, the amount of trash in landfills would be greatly reduced.

The United States produces 1,600 pounds of trash per person each year—more than any other country in the world. Recycling an object costs about half as much as sending it to a landfill. So recycling is better for the environment and it saves money.

CHANGE STARTS AT HOME

This house has been turned into an eco haven. Can you spot the six things that have been changed?

Eco-homes use much less energy because they have features that are less wasteful, such as double-paned windows and insulation to keep in heat.

Some people now choose to live in "tiny houses," which are exceptionally small and compact. They are very good for the environment because they require much less energy to heat. Also, fewer belongings can fit inside them, which keeps the owner from buying lots of things that they don't need.

Rainwater harvesting is a method of collecting water to be used at a later time. Water drains from the rooftop into the gutter, and then it is collected and stored in a barrel. The harvested water can be used for watering the garden or washing the car.

83

SPOT SPOTTING

Can you find the identical cats? Match up the six pairs of Amur leopards in the picture below.

1.

2.

3.

4.

5.

6.

7.

8.

9.

10.

11.

12.

It is estimated that only ninety adult Amur leopards are living today, making them critically endangered. Hunters want to catch them for their beautiful fur, which sells for high prices.

The Amur leopard lives in eastern Russia and China. These areas have extremely cold winters, so the leopard has fur that can grow up to 3 inches long to keep it warm.

84

SEWER SPRINT

These pesky pipes have sprung a leak and are wasting valuable water. Find your way through the pipe maze below to fix the problem pipe. Cross over and duck under the bridges to help you reach the leak in record time. The example shows you how this works.

EXAMPLE

The red line is the path.

UNDER A BRIDGE   OVER A BRIDGE

Moving water to our homes uses energy and costs money. To save water, turn off the tap when brushing your teeth, take shorter showers, and only run your washing machine when it's full.

Some clever people have found a way to use water to create energy at home. By attaching turbines to their water supply they are able to create their own hydroelectric power.

START

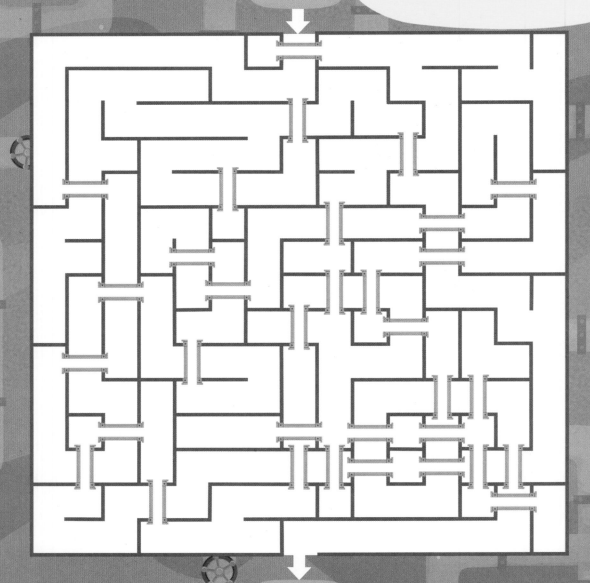

FINISH

WHERE DOES FOOD COME FROM?

Do you know how food is made? Match the food items to the things that they are made from below.

Meat production contributes more to climate change than cars and planes combined. Approximately 3,000 gallons of water are needed to create just one hamburger.

TOMATOES

CHOCOLATE

FRIES

POTATOES

OMELETTE

CHEESE

HUMMUS

CHICKPEAS

MILK

COCOA BEANS

Food can travel great distances before it ends up on your plate. For example, bananas are normally grown in the warmest places on Earth, but they can be bought in almost any country.

KETCHUP

EGGS

ALL THE FUN OF THE FAIR

Lots of people have been to the fairground, and there's trash everywhere. Guide the girl along the path to collect all the trash, avoiding the people who are in the way. When she reaches the finish, write how many of each type of trash she has collected above the correct bin.

KEY

TICKETS

JUICE BOXES

PLASTIC BOTTLES

COTTON CANDY

START

Litter is waste or trash that is disposed of in any place it doesn't belong. Something as small as chewing gum or as large as a washing machine can be litter. The most common type of litter is fast-food packaging.

FINISH

Litter that works its way
to the ocean creates a toxic
environment for many creatures.
Marine animals can be killed
if they become entangled
in or eat litter.

SAFARI SPOTTING

In a national reserve in Africa, this busy watering hole is full of thirsty animals that have stopped for a drink. Count how many of each animal you spot from the checklist, then add up your answers. Does your total match the one shown?

CHECKLIST

ZEBRAS

SECRETARY BIRDS

LEOPARD TORTOISES

SNAKES

STRIPED POLECATS

FLAMINGOS

TOTAL = 26

Humans are currently the biggest threat to animals in Africa. Poachers are people who illegally hunt animals for sport or money. Elephants and tigers are just some of the animals that are hunted for their tusks or skins, and are now endangered.

When done in a safe and respectful way, visiting a national reserve for a vacation is great for the wildlife. Tourists bring money to the area, allowing animals to be protected. It also discourages poachers from hunting the animals.

WHAT'S HIDING IN THE GARDEN?

Complete this dot-to-dot puzzle to find out
which creature is hiding in the garden.

I eat nuts that I collect and hide in
the ground to feast on later. When I
forget to dig the nuts up again, they
can sometimes grow into trees.

I am very smart. To stop my food from being stolen by
other creatures, I sometimes pretend to bury my collection,
but actually hide them in other places. This confuses any
animals that have been spying on me.

A BLESSING OF NARWHALS

A group of narwhals is called a blessing. How many narwhals can you find in the blessing below?

Narwhals are sea mammals that live in the cold waters of the Arctic. They are sometimes known as "unicorns of the sea" because of the large tooth that the males have. It grows right through their upper lip and can reach 9 feet in length.

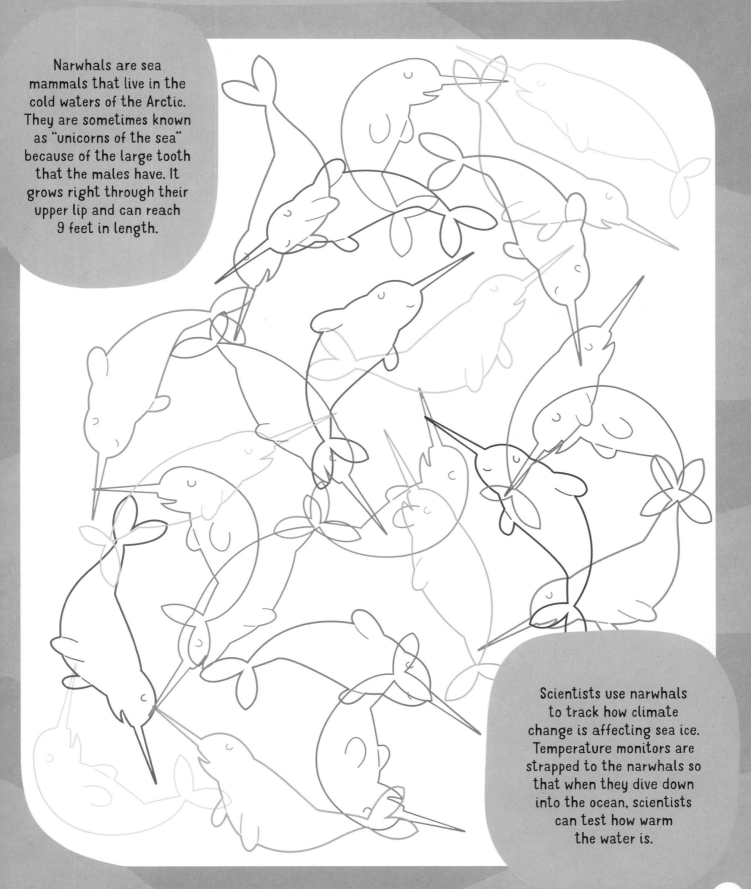

Scientists use narwhals to track how climate change is affecting sea ice. Temperature monitors are strapped to the narwhals so that when they dive down into the ocean, scientists can test how warm the water is.

LEMUR LOOKOUT

This jungle is teeming with ring-tailed lemurs who all look very alike. Read the clues below to find Lucinda Lemur in the picture. You will have to be eagle-eyed as she is quite shy.

CLUES

Lucinda has:

1. Black circles around her eyes
2. A baby lemur clinging to her back
3. A white patch on her right arm
4. Twelve black stripes on her tail

Ring-tailed lemurs are found on the island of Madagascar off the east coast of Africa. They live in groups called troops, and babies stay with their mothers for about 2 years after they are born.

Habitat destruction is the biggest threat to ring-tailed lemurs in Madagascar. Over 80 percent of the forest has been destroyed due to the harvesting of wood and clearing of land for farming.

THE VIEW FROM SPACE

There are thousands of satellites that orbit Earth to keep an eye on what is going on. Look at the image below and the pictures on the opposite page. Can you figure out which satellite took each picture?

A.

B.

C.

D.

E.

F.

Satellites orbiting the Earth have many different jobs, from allowing people to make long-distance calls to monitoring gases in the atmosphere. They keep track of wildfires and the ice caps, and help scientists predict the weather and climate.

AN ICE CAP

A STORM

RAIN FOREST

Phytoplankton are tiny organisms (single-celled life forms) that live in water. When there is enough sunlight and nutrients available to them, they reproduce and become so numerous that they change the color of the water. This is called a "bloom" and can be seen from space.

PHYTOPLANKTON IN THE OCEAN

PENGUIN POOP

A DESERT

Satellite images of Antarctica show penguin poop, also known as guano. By studying images of penguin guano, scientists can see where penguins are decreasing in numbers.

TIME TO RECHARGE

Circle the group below that has all of the parts that you need to make this picture of an electric car and charging station.

The majority of air pollution in developed countries is caused by traffic. Electric vehicles like this one do not produce any exhaust emissions, unlike fossil fuel-powered vehicles, so they reduce air pollution.

Some electric cars, called "hybrids," are powered by both electricity and fossil fuels. Many of them have battery packs, which charge as the cars move. The cars then switch between energy sources, resulting in lower carbon emissions.

A.

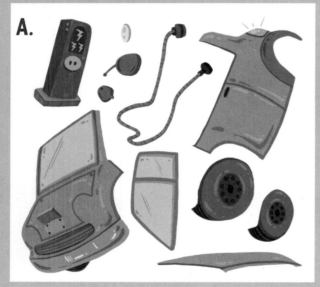

B.

C.

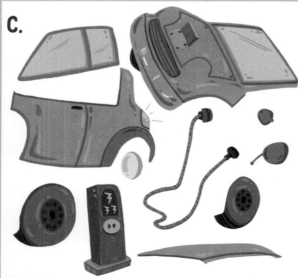

D.

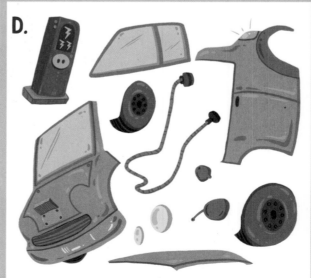

TIMETABLE TROUBLE

Don't be late to catch the train! Check the time and look at the departures board below, then answer the questions.

Trains only give out half the amount of carbon dioxide emitted by airplanes. Per person, they also emit just a quarter of the greenhouse gases of a car.

STATION

Clock: 11:15

TIME	DEPARTURES
11:40	MAIN STREET
11:43	FERN ROAD
11:50	FOREST STREET
11:59	POND STREET
12:00	GREEN PARK LANE
12:05	WILLOW BROOK
12:12	ROWAN LANE
12:25	WARREN STREET
12:40	BURROW ROAD
1:00	BIRCH LANE

Electric trains use electricity to operate rather than diesel fuel. The electricity can come from any source—from fossil fuels to renewable energies, such as solar or wind power.

QUESTIONS

1. If you want to go to Main Street, how long do you have until your train leaves?
2. The train to Main Street arrives there at 12:30. How long will your journey be?
3. The train to Pond Street takes 40 minutes. What time will it arrive?
4. You've just missed a train to Forest Street. How long do you have to wait for the next one?
5. The train to Warren Street is delayed by 19 minutes. What time will it leave?

EVERYDAY ECO SWAPS

Many items are made to be used just once, but this creates waste and is bad for the environment. Follow the rules to draw lines in the grid below and connect the single-use items with their eco-friendly alternatives.

KEY

PLASTIC BAG – FABRIC TOTE BAG

PLASTIC TOOTHBRUSH – BAMBOO TOOTHBRUSH

PLASTIC STRAW – METAL STRAW

PLASTIC WATER BOTTLE – REUSABLE METAL WATER BOTTLE

PLASTIC SHOWER GEL BOTTLE – BAR OF SOAP

PLASTIC FORK – WOODEN FORK

PAPER TOWEL – FABRIC CLOTH

PLASTIC SANDWICH BAG – STEEL LUNCH BOX

BATTERIES – RECHARGEABLE BATTERIES

RULES

1. The lines must not cross or touch each other.
2. Lines can only go through each square once.
3. You cannot use diagonal lines.

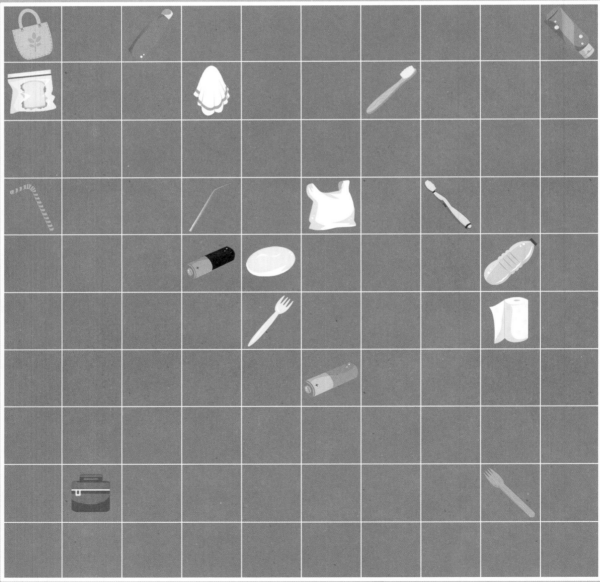

Plastic bag fees have been introduced in many stores to reduce usage. This tiny change has made a big difference and now people use far fewer plastic bags each year.

PICK UP STRAWS

Take a look at the eight paper straws that have been dropped
in a pile below, then answer the three questions about them.

QUESTIONS

1. How many paper straws would you need to move to pick up the blue straw,
without disturbing the ones underneath?
2. What color is the fourth paper straw from the top?
3. How many paper straws are under the orange paper straw?

Around 390 million
plastic straws are used in
the United States every
day. Many of them end up
in the oceans, harming
seabirds, turtles, and
other marine life.

Paper straws are a great
eco-friendly alternative to
plastic straws. They are
marine biodegradable,
which means they can
break down in the oceans
without causing harm.

Plastic straws should be
recyclable, but most of
them are too lightweight to
be properly sorted by the
mechanical recycler. This
means that they fall through
sorting screens and can end
up in a landfill.

FEEDING FRENZY

In the ocean, microscopic creatures are eaten by fish, and those fish are eaten by even bigger creatures. This is called a food chain. Choose the correct options from the box along the bottom of the page to complete the food chains. An example has been completed for you, and there are clues in case you get stuck.

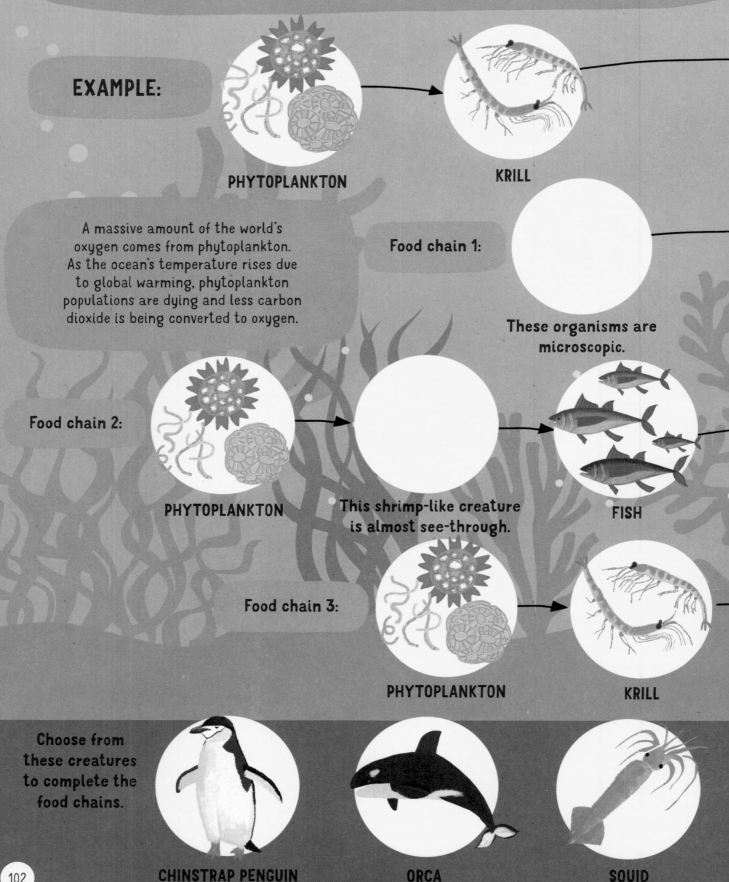

EXAMPLE:

PHYTOPLANKTON

KRILL

A massive amount of the world's oxygen comes from phytoplankton. As the ocean's temperature rises due to global warming, phytoplankton populations are dying and less carbon dioxide is being converted to oxygen.

Food chain 1:

These organisms are microscopic.

Food chain 2:

PHYTOPLANKTON

This shrimp-like creature is almost see-through.

FISH

Food chain 3:

PHYTOPLANKTON

KRILL

Choose from these creatures to complete the food chains.

CHINSTRAP PENGUIN

ORCA

SQUID

Ocean food chains begin with phytoplankton or other organisms that get their energy from the Sun, and end with large sea creatures, such as sharks. The animals at the top are called apex predators. When phytoplankton die, they sink to the bottom of lakes and oceans, where they are preserved in soil. Scientists use these phytoplankton to study how the climate has changed over time.

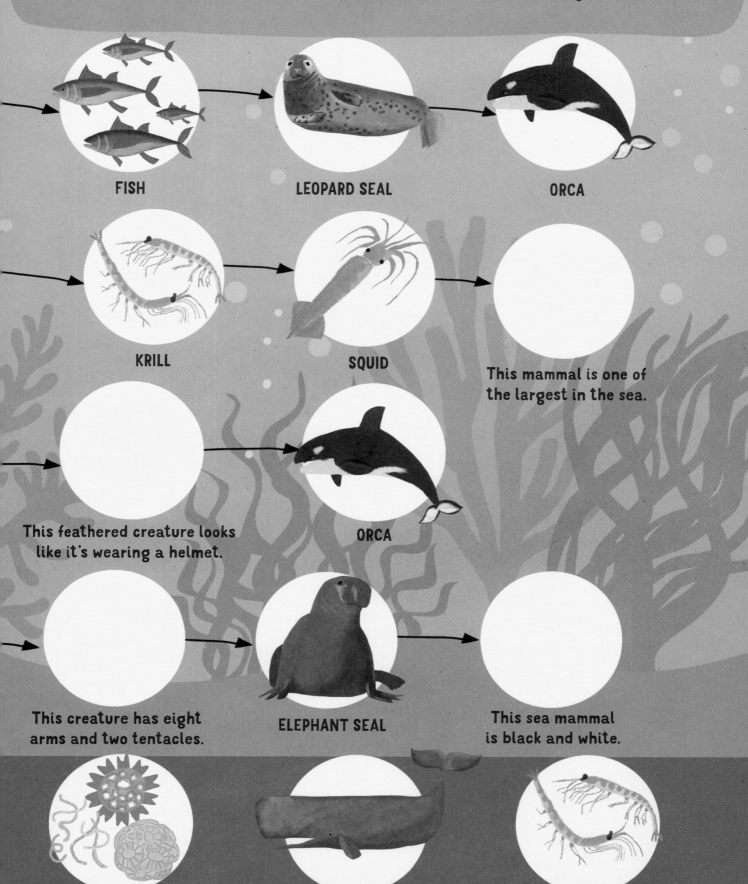

FISH

LEOPARD SEAL

ORCA

KRILL

SQUID

This mammal is one of the largest in the sea.

This feathered creature looks like it's wearing a helmet.

ORCA

This creature has eight arms and two tentacles.

ELEPHANT SEAL

This sea mammal is black and white.

PHYTOPLANKTON

SPERM WHALE

KRILL

GREENHOUSE GAS GLOBETROTTING

For this game you will need a marker for each player, a dice, and a timer. Roll the dice and move your marker clockwise around the globe, following the instructions that you land on. The winner is the first person to get around the board three times.

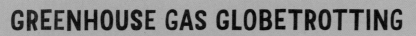

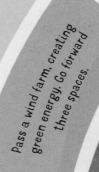

Pass a wind farm, creating green energy. Go forward three spaces.

You take a refillable bottle out with you instead of buying a plastic bottle of water. Go forward one space.

You pass a forest that has been cut down. There are no longer trees to absorb carbon dioxide and release oxygen. Go back three spaces.

Greenhouse gases surround the Earth, trapping heat from the Sun and keeping the planet warm. This is called the greenhouse effect. Without it, the Earth would be as cold as outer space and life on our planet wouldn't exist.

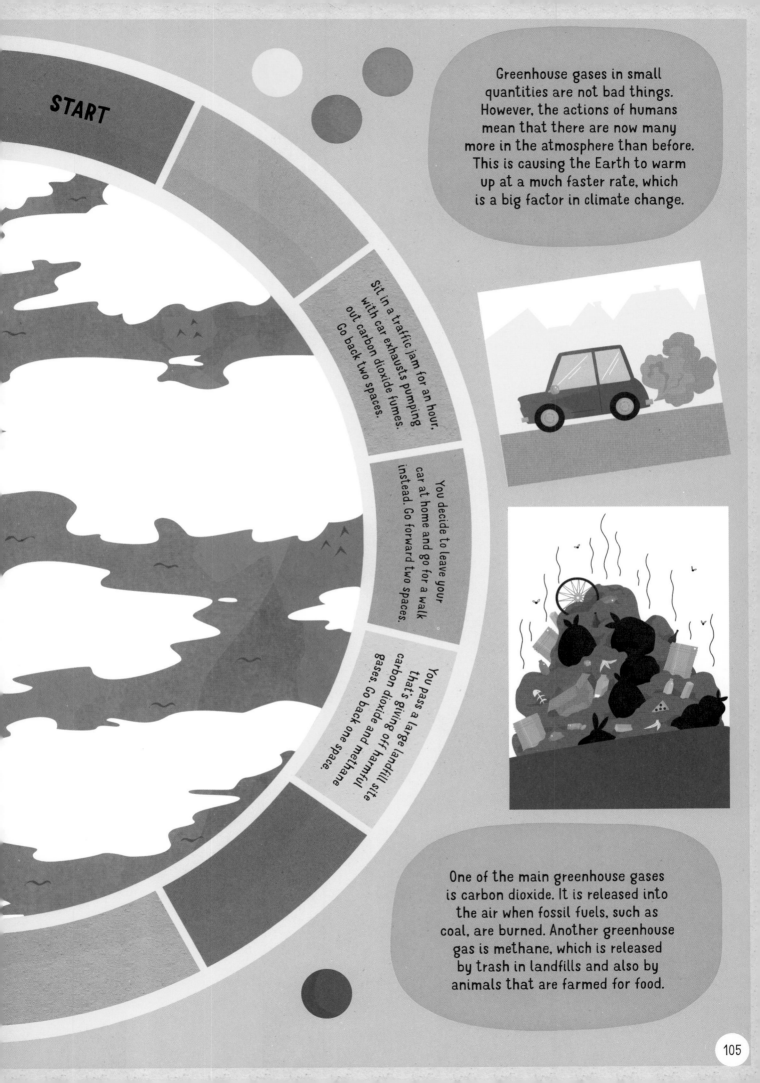

START

Sit in a traffic jam for an hour, with car exhausts pumping out carbon dioxide fumes. Go back two spaces.

You decide to leave your car at home and go for a walk instead. Go forward two spaces.

You pass a large landfill site that's giving off harmful gases, carbon dioxide and methane gases. Go back one space.

Greenhouse gases in small quantities are not bad things. However, the actions of humans mean that there are now many more in the atmosphere than before. This is causing the Earth to warm up at a much faster rate, which is a big factor in climate change.

One of the main greenhouse gases is carbon dioxide. It is released into the air when fossil fuels, such as coal, are burned. Another greenhouse gas is methane, which is released by trash in landfills and also by animals that are farmed for food.

BUGS FOR BREAKFAST

These creepy-crawlies may not look appetizing but they make for a healthy meal. Can you draw three straight lines on each plate to divide it into four areas? Each area needs to contain one of each type of bug.

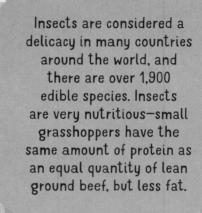

Insects are considered a delicacy in many countries around the world, and there are over 1,900 edible species. Insects are very nutritious—small grasshoppers have the same amount of protein as an equal quantity of lean ground beef, but less fat.

Each area must contain **1** black ant, **1** mealworm, and **1** grasshopper.

Each area must contain **1** dung beetle, **1** cricket, and **1** caterpillar.

Each area must contain **1** locust, **1** scorpion, and **1** cockroach.

Raising insects to eat is very green. They take much less land and food to farm than is needed for cows, pigs, or sheep.

WHAT'S FOR DINNER?

It's time to cook up a storm in the kitchen. Read the recipes below and figure out which one uses up all the ingredients shown, leaving no food wasted.

KEY

BABY SWEET CORN

RED PEPPER

GARLIC

MUSHROOM

SNAP PEA

GREEN ONION

STIR-FRY 1

12 snap peas
1 red pepper
4 baby sweet corns
3 cloves of garlic
4 mushrooms
3 green onions

STIR-FRY 2

1 clove of garlic
10 snap peas
3 green onions
1 red pepper
4 baby sweet corns
6 mushrooms

STIR-FRY 3

4 baby sweet corns
12 snap peas
1 red pepper
3 green onions
1 clove of garlic
6 mushrooms

An astonishing one-third of all food that is produced around the world is wasted each year. The amount of food that is thrown away in rich countries is almost equal to the total amount of food produced in the large area of land that lies south of the Sahara Desert in Africa.

Supermarkets will throw food away because it doesn't look perfect, even if it's absolutely fine to eat. An "ugly food" movement is working to save produce from waste and sell it for cheaper prices. Keep an eye out for "wonky" vegetables in your local supermarket.

RAIN FOREST RUMBLE

The temperature is rising in this rain forest, and lots of animals have decided to visit the waterfall to cool off. Which tiles at the bottom of the page cannot be found in the picture?

Jaguars are perfectly suited to life in the rain forest. Unlike many other felines, they do not shy away from water and are actually very good swimmers. Sadly, their rain forest homes are quickly disappearing. They can only be found in less than half the places that they lived in previously.

A.

B.

C.

D.

Rain forests are important to the world's water cycle. Trees release water from their leaves into the atmosphere. This forms rain clouds. When rain forests are cut down there is not as much moisture being released into the air, and this can lead to droughts.

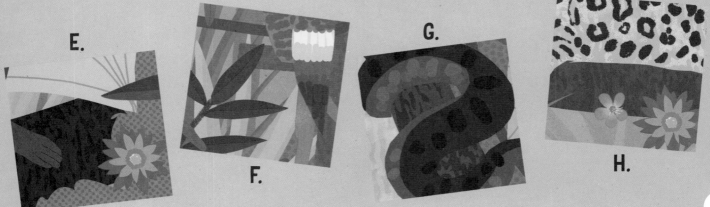

E.

F.

G.

H.

CLASSROOM CRAFTS

The children from this class have brought in their reuse projects. They have all turned a piece of trash into something new. Can you spot all of the items of junk that they used in the classroom?

PLASTIC BOTTLE PLANTERS

SOCK MONKEY

Reuse is often confused with recycling. Recycling a material is breaking it down to make something new, while reusing an item is lengthening its life by fixing it or finding a new use for it.

TIC-TAC-TOE

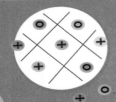

EGG CARTON CATERPILLAR

CUP AND STRAW
PINWHEELS

WRAPPING PAPER
BEAD NECKLACE

By reusing items
instead of buying
new ones, you are
preventing pollution,
saving energy, and
reducing greenhouse
gases that contribute
to climate change.

TIN CAN WIND CHIMES

T-SHIRT SHOPPING BAG

Remember: one person's
trash is another person's
treasure! Borrowing or
swapping gently used
items with friends or
neighbors can cut down
on waste and help you to
save money.

GLASS JAR SNOW GLOBE

CARDBOARD CASTLE

HOW ECO-FRIENDLY ARE YOU?

So, you think you're an eco-warrior? Take this test to find out. Answer all the questions below, then color in four footsteps for every question that you answer "yes" to. The more footsteps you collect, the more eco-friendly you are.

1. Do you turn the tap off when you brush your teeth?
2. Do you turn the lights off when you leave a room?
3. Do you put plastic bottles in the recycling bin?
4. Do you walk, cycle, or carpool to school?
5. Do you say "no thanks" when offered a plastic straw for your drink?

"Carbon footprint" is a term used to show how much carbon dioxide is produced by your regular activities. Activities such as how you get to school or whether you turn off the light when you leave the room can affect the size of your carbon footprint.

START

WELL DONE, YOU'VE STARTED YOUR ECO JOURNEY.

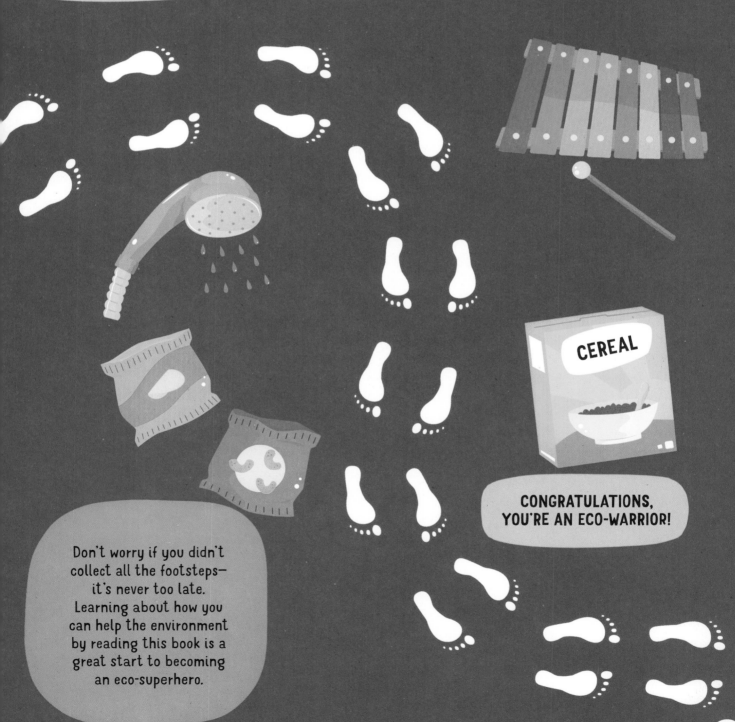

6. Do you save leftover food to eat later?
7. Do you keep showers short to save water?
8. Do you give old toys to charity rather than putting them in the trash?
9. Do you use trash or old things for craft projects?
10. Do you always put trash in the trash can rather than littering?

EXCELLENT, KEEP UP THE GREAT WORK!

While China has the largest carbon footprint of all the countries in the world, Qatar has the largest per person. Belize and Bermuda are among the countries that have the smallest carbon footprints.

CONGRATULATIONS, YOU'RE AN ECO-WARRIOR!

Don't worry if you didn't collect all the footsteps—it's never too late. Learning about how you can help the environment by reading this book is a great start to becoming an eco-superhero.

CEREAL

THE BIG GREEN QUIZ

1. What is the name for an energy source that will never run out?

   a. Everlasting
   b. Renewable
   c. Fossil fuel

2. Which word describes when a bee transfers pollen from one flower to another?

   a. Delivery
   b. Gift
   c. Pollination

3. How much of the world's fresh water is contained in Arctic ice?

   a. 10 percent
   b. 50 percent
   c. 100 percent

4. What is currently the biggest threat to coral reefs?

   a. Sharks
   b. Humans
   c. Tidal waves

5. What is the name for a person who illegally hunts animals or fish?

   a. A poacher
   b. A tourist
   c. A birder

6. Which of the following is not a greenhouse gas?

   a. Carbon dioxide
   b. Methane
   c. Nitrogen

7. What does the "e" in e-waste stand for?

   a. Electricity
   b. Electronic
   c. Energy

8. What is the name for a huge mass of ice that flows across the land like a river?

a. Ocean
b. Glacier
c. Iceberg

9. Roughly how much of the food that is produced for humans to eat is wasted each year?

a. One-third
b. One-half
c. All of it

10. What do plants make that humans need?

a. Leaves
b. Oxygen
c. Sugar

11. What do most ocean food chains start with?

a. Phytoplankton
b. A predator
c. Fish

12. What is the term used for the amount of carbon dioxide that a person creates from their regular activities?

a. Carbon handprint
b. Carbon emissions
c. Carbon footprint

13. Where do discarded plastic straws end up?

a. In landfills
b. In the ocean
c. Both of the above

14. What is the term for when more fish are caught than can be replaced in the ocean?

a. Overfishing
b. Pole and line fishing
c. Farming

15. Which animal's home is being destroyed to make room for oil palm tree plantations?

a. Squirrels
b. Orangutans
c. Pangolins

ALL THE ANSWERS

ECO ISLAND P4–5

1. Deer
2. Five
3. Twenty-six
4. East
5. Six
6. Three

NECTAR DELIVERY P6

HONEY HUNT P7

A. Black-eyed Susan
B. Violet
C. Catmint

FOLLOW THE TRACKS P8–9

A. White-tailed deer
B. Rattlesnake
C. Grizzly bear
D. Snowshoe hare
E. Red squirrel
F. Mallard duck

RAIN FOREST RESIDENTS P10

6 monstera leaves
3 macaw parrots
18 cocoa pods
12 orchids
4 poison dart frogs
Total = 43

FIND THE FOSSIL FUEL P11

1. Coal is formed when PLANTS die. They become buried in the ground and squashed into ROCK.
2. Around 80% of the world's energy comes from fossil fuels.
3. Natural gas has no smell but can be dangerous. A substance called mercaptan is added to it to make it smell like ROTTEN EGGS, so it is easier to detect.
4. At the rate that humans are currently using it up, it is estimated that the reserves of OIL will run out by the year 2052.
5. The burning of fossil fuels for energy releases CARBON DIOXIDE, which causes global warming.

6. Nuclear power stations generate cheap energy but are very expensive to build. They also create dangerous RADIOACTIVE WASTE.
7. Oil is formed by plankton, ALGAE and other matter that sank and was buried at the bottom of the ocean.
8. Crude oil is used to make GASOLINE.
9. In America, NATURAL GAS is the fuel that is most often used to produce electricity.
10. SOLAR POWER is a renewable energy source, which means it will never run out.

CORAL REEF HIDE-AND-SEEK P16–17

5 leafy sea dragons
4 lionfish
8 sea fan corals
8 garden eels
12 Christmas tree worms
4 mimic octopuses
6 trumpetfish
Total = 47

RECYCLING BINGO P12–13

WHAT'S HIDING IN THE RAIN FOREST? P18

It's an orangutan.

TEAMWORK TWINS P14

1 and 8
2 and 11
3 and 9
4 and 10
5 and 13
6 and 12
7 and 14

PLUMBING PRO P19

A. 7
B. 1
C. 2
D. 3
E. 5

FLOWER POWER P20–21

GOING CAMPING P22

Group C contains all the correct parts.

TENT TROUBLE P23

GREEDY WORM P24–25

PATCHWORK FASHION P26

The stripy underwear hasn't been used.

SHOPPING SPREE P27

1. $4.
2. Four items: the hat, the blue sweater, the orange-and-yellow top, and the green T-shirt.
3. No, you would be 50 cents short.

SCHOOL CARPOOL P28–29

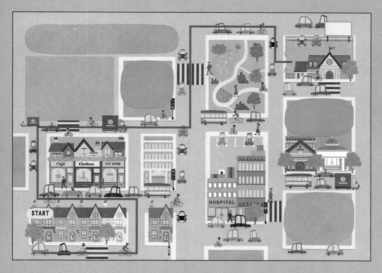

1. There are five houses on your street (including house number five).
2. You drive past seven bikes on your way to school.
3. The toy store is two doors down from the café.
4. There are five ducks in the pond.
5. There are three buses

TURBINE TEST P30

1. Fourteen
2. Five
3. Red
4. Three
5. Flowers

WASTE OF ENERGY P31

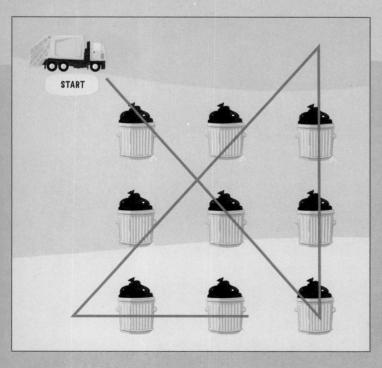

HURRY HATCHLINGS P32

ODD TURTLES OUT P33

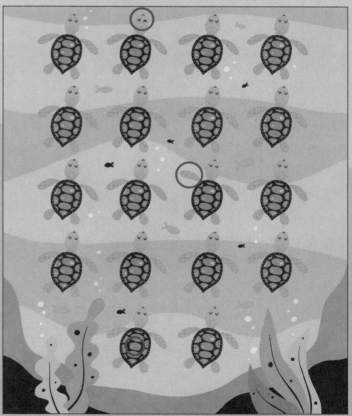

MISSION TO SPACE P34–35

2. You find a glove.
3. The coordinates of this square are B5 and you collect a spatula.
4. You need to move two squares down to collect the nuts and bolts.
5. You have not collected the video camera, and it is in square C6.

SEED SHUFFLE P36

A. Pumpkin seeds
B. Pine cone from a pine tree
C. Acorns from an oak tree
D. Sunflower seeds
E. Maple tree seeds, called "samaras"
F. Poppy seeds

GARDEN GRIDS P37

1.

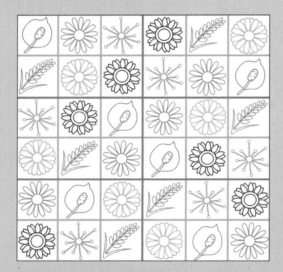

2.

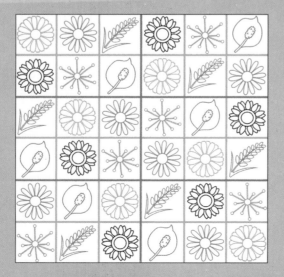

SOLAR SCRIBBLES P38–39

There should be twenty solar panels with stars on, four with circles on, twelve with swirls on, and four left blank.

ON YOUR MARKS . . . P40–41

A. 3rd
B. 4th
C. 1st
D. 2nd

AMAZING ARCTIC P42–43

Images B, C, F, G, and J are in the scene.

FROG HOPPING P44

BUSY BEAVER P45

There are thirty-six sticks in the dam.

FRESH FOOD FEAST P46–47

1. You would get $3.50 in change.
2. This would all cost $11, so you would not be able to buy some flowers as you would be $1 short.
3. It would cost $9.70 to buy all of those items.

POLAR BEAR REFLECTIONS P48

Reflection C is correct.

EGG COUNT P49

There will be twenty-one eggs.

MUSEUM MEMORY MUDDLE P53

The Tecopa pupfish is swimming the other way.

WHO HOOKED THE BOOT? P54

D hooked the boot.

ODD FISH OUT P55

CROSSED WIRES P56–57

A. 2
B. 5
C. 6
D. 1
E. 4
F. 3

SILHOUETTE SPOTTING P58

A. Birch
B. Hawthorn
C. Poplar
D. Beech
E. Oak
F. Maple

ANCIENT TREES P59

D is the oldest tree.

1. The youngest tree is 2,327 years old.
2. The second-oldest tree is 4,678 years old.

VEGGIE PATCH VISITORS P60-61

12 rabbits
3 snails
4 slugs
3 ladybugs
4 crows
Total = 26

RECYCLED ROBOT P62

Group A contains all the correct parts.

E-WASTE ENIGMA P63

1.

2.

STAR TO STAR P64-65

The names of the constellations are:
Red (example) = Cassiopeia
Pink = Orion
Purple = Ursa Minor, aka Little Dipper
Green = Pegasus
Orange = Taurus
Yellow = Scorpius

PLASTIC POLLUTION P66

There are eighteen plastic bottles in the image.

CREEPY-CRAWLY CAPER P67

6 stag beetles
8 spiders
6 ladybugs
3 centipedes
6 golden stag beetles
5 dung beetles
7 cucumber beetles
7 fruit beetles
Total = 48

FUN IN THE SNOW P71

KANGAROO CROSSING P72–73

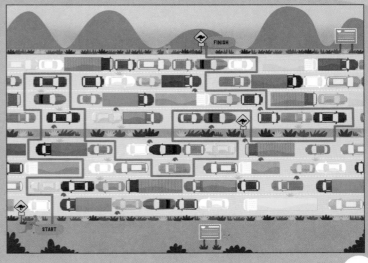

BREAKAWAY ICEBERG P70

D is the iceberg that fits in the gap.

SPOTTER'S GUIDE P74–75

A. Wood thrush
B. Rose-breasted grosbeak
C. Northern cardinal
D. White-breasted nuthatch
E. Purple finch
F. Blue jay

ON THE FARM P76–77

Tiles A, D, F, H, and I are not in the scene.

ABOVE OR UNDERGROUND? P78

Broccoli—aboveground
Chickpeas—aboveground, in pods from bushy plants
Carrots—underground, but the leaves grow aboveground
Cashew nuts—aboveground, they grow off the bottom of a fruit called a cashew apple
Peanuts—underground, the flowers grow above-ground and a peg (or stem) grows down from the plant into the ground; the peanut grows on the end of the peg and is encased in a hard, protective shell
Pineapples—aboveground, they grow on a stem from a plant that has long, thin leaves
Potatoes—underground, but the leaves grow aboveground
Radishes—underground, but the leaves grow aboveground
Watermelons—aboveground, they grow on a vine-like plant and rest on the ground because they are so heavy

THINK LIKE AN APE P79

1. B – Their physical similarity to humans is recognized in this name.
2. A – When orangutans eat fruit and berries, the seeds are passed through their digestive systems and then fall to the forest floor (in their poop), where they begin to grow.
3. C – The Tapanuli orangutan was identified in 2017. The other two species are the Sumatran and Bornean orangutans.

4. A – They can take up to twenty years to grow, but the strongest, healthiest males all develop these extraordinary facial features, called flanges.
5. C – As well as carrying their not-so-young offspring around the forest, mothers feed them milk for up to five years and sleep in a nest with them every night until a new baby is born.
6. C – Although they can walk and use their long arms to swing, orangutans spend most of their time resting in the forest trees.
7. C – Palm oil is used in all sorts of different foods and everyday products, including pizza, cookies, makeup, soap, margarine, and hand soap. Read the labels of the things you buy that contain palm oil to make sure that it has been farmed sustainably, or avoid buying them altogether.

Scores:
6–7 – Amazing. You're a true king of the swingers.
3–5 – Nearly there. Why not try again and you'll be top of the tree.
0–2 – Oops. Stop monkeying around and give the quiz another try.

WHAT A LOAD OF GARBAGE P80–81

9 hair spray cans
6 batteries
7 aluminum cans
2 televisions
5 old car tires
3 coffee makers
Total = 32

CHANGE STARTS AT HOME P82–83

1. Solar panels
2. Double-paned windows
3. Water barrel and watering can
4. Vegetable patch
5. Recycling bins
6. Electric car

SPOT SPOTTING P84

1 and 7
2 and 10
3 and 8
4 and 12
5 and 11
6 and 9

TERMITE TONGUE TWISTER P85

The termites in chambers D and E add up to forty.

SEWER SPRINT P86

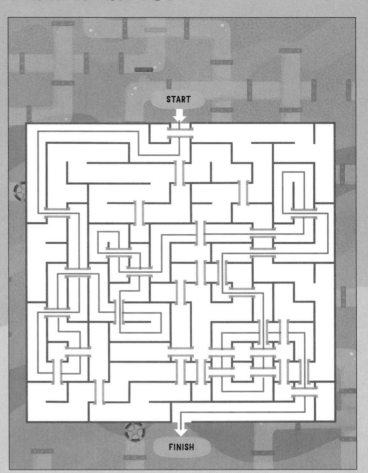

WHERE DOES FOOD COME FROM? P87

Ketchup – tomatoes
Chocolate – cocoa beans
Fries – potatoes
Omelette – eggs
Hummus – chickpeas
Cheese – milk

ALL THE FUN OF THE FAIR P88–89

There are five tickets, six plastic bottles, five juice boxes, and five sticks of cotton candy.

SAFARI SPOTTING P90–91

- **4** zebras
- **2** secretary birds
- **5** leopard tortoises
- **4** snakes
- **5** striped polecats
- **6** flamingos
- **Total = 26**

A BLESSING OF NARWHALS P93

There are twenty-four narwhals in the jumble.

LEMUR LOOKOUT P94–95

WHAT'S HIDING IN THE GARDEN? P92

It's a squirrel.

THE VIEW FROM SPACE P96–97

- **A.** An ice cap
- **B.** Phytoplankton in the ocean
- **C.** A storm
- **D.** Penguin poop
- **E.** Rain forest
- **F.** A desert

TIME TO RECHARGE P98

Group D contains the correct parts.

TIMETABLE TROUBLE P99

1. 25 minutes
2. 50 minutes
3. 12:39
4. 35 minutes
5. 12:44

EVERYDAY ECO SWAPS P100

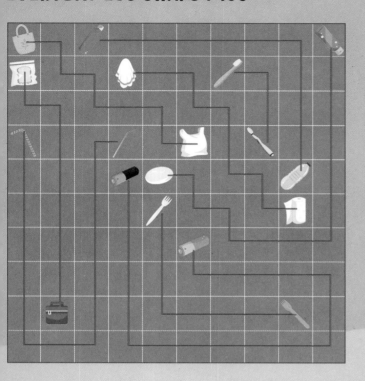

BUGS FOR BREAKFAST P106

Tiles A, B, and H are not in the image.

PICK UP STRAWS P101

1. You would need to move two straws—the gray one and the green one.
2. The fourth straw from the top is pink.
3. Only one straw is underneath the orange one—the red straw is at the bottom of the pile.

WHAT'S FOR DINNER? P107

Stir-fry number 3 has all the correct ingredients.

FEEDING FRENZY P102–103

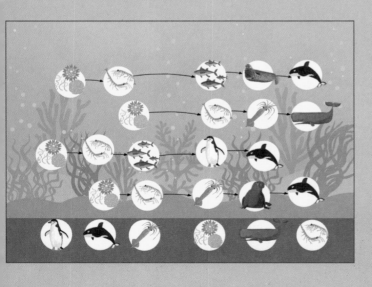

RAIN FOREST RUMBLE P108–109

Tiles A, B, and H are not in the image.

CLASSROOM CRAFTS P110–11

THE BIG GREEN QUIZ P114–115

1. B – Renewable
2. C – Pollination
3. A – 10 percent
4. B – Humans
5. A – A poacher
6. C – Nitrogen
7. B – Electronic
8. B – Glacier
9. A – One-third
10. B – Oxygen
11. A – Phytoplankton
12. C – Carbon footprint
13. C – Both of the above
14. A – Overfishing
15. B – Orangutans